CHIN UP

*How putting down our phones
can open our eyes and ready our feet
to walk in God's purpose*

KENNAN BUCKNER

Marken Media Co. LLC
© 2020

chinupthebook.com
facebook.com/groups/chinupthebook

Cover images by The Girl Behind the Lens/Minerva Wallace

ISBN: 978-0-578-75631-8

First Edition: August 2020

10 9 8 7 6 5 4 3 2 1

CHAPTERS

To my husband Marcus, my gift from our Good Father. Thank you for believing in me. There's nothing that can stop this cord of three strands.

INTRODUCTION

The book you have in your hands is kind of a miracle. Though I'm Type A, the firstborn, a finisher by nature, and a planner by God's good plan, I find myself *quitting* when I can't wrap my head around a feasible plan for accomplishing a ginormous task such as writing a book. I can't tell you how many books I've started and stopped the past several years. What you are holding is a miracle. This book is the wonderful, glorious exception.

About a year ago, when praying about writing a book, the Lord told me *You've already written one.* I have been a journal writer and attempted poet since my early teens, taking notes at Bible studies, writing prayers, poems, and songs. I grabbed on to God's thought and ran with it with several frenzied (and very late) evenings at the dining room table, trying to decipher which lessons I'd learned over the years that I should share. And you can probably tell. This is not that book. With overwhelm and angst, I quit again.

With three kids under the age of five, a brand-new business, serving as a leader for MOPS (Mothers of Preschoolers), and keeping up with regular responsibilities, I chalked up quitting to another "now is not the season to write a book" moment and moved on.

Then another gracious reminder and another challenge. As I am typing this, we are under the COVID-19 quarantine. Texans, like the rest of the citizens of this country and world, are told to avoid non-essential travel. Businesses, libraries, Mother's Day Out programs, and playgrounds are closed; if you're a mom, you're catching my hints! We are three weeks into this slower, can't-go-anywhere pace. My husband and I aren't in a financial panic, but just as things were ramping up in 2020 in our business, we can now say things are not busy.

Again the still, small voice, *I have given you this time. Write.*

My husband is at home with our kids (Jaxson age four, Caden age two, and Emilyn age nine months) while I'm holed up in our office, more ready than ever to share what I have shared in small, bitesize pieces with my fellow MOPS moms over the past three years. I did not know it then, but I know it now. This book is what He meant with the assurance *you've already written one.*

Chin Up is not only the cheery encouragement to press on, but it is also the rally cry to cling to the truth called the Bible. Pray hard. Trust God. It started with the phrase "Chin up, phone down" in our house when I would challenge my husband to put down his iPhone and engage with our firstborn son and me. Being the graphic designer he is, he turned it into a shirt we sold to friends, family, and strangers at a few area vendor markets. People were catching on, and the message was relatable and resounding.

Today, *Chin Up* is the theme I see carried through each of the chapters of this book, the overarching theme of everything God has been showing me about Himself. With my phone down, eyes open, and feet ready, I can walk in God's purpose. I know Who I belong to, I celebrate the unique calling God has placed on my life, and I find community when I choose to live with authenticity, enjoy each gift, and love Jesus. I hope this book leaves you challenged, encouraged, and feeling loved because you are so very dearly loved.

PHONE DOWN
NO MORE FEAR
OF MISSING OUT

For the Lord God is a sun and shield; the Lord bestows favor and honor. No good thing does he withhold from those who walk uprightly. – Psalm 84:11

GREW UP WITH LIMITED ACCESS TO THE INTERNET, back when you had to use dial-up. In junior high and high school, I wasn't allowed to have a MySpace account, but I did share an email account with my Dad.

9

I am sure those messages were fascinating. What would a preteen have to say to friends she'd seen a few hours before at school?

When I was in college, friends introduced me to a relatively new thing called Facebook. My roommate Jessica and our friend Sarah showed me how to set up my profile, and off we were to the land of stalking fellow University of Mary Hardin-Baylor singles.

Social media became a part of my daily life, a sort of living journal and scrapbook. Then nine years later, in December 2016, I did something pretty radical for me. I limited my access to social media. I removed the apps from my phone. After having a baby, choosing to stay home, leaving a job I loved, and losing my circle of work friends, social media was not a healthy outlet.

I did something crazy. Not only did I take social media apps off my phone, but I had my husband Marcus block them from the Safari app (because I would look up their websites).

So for a whole year, my one source for social media was on a desktop computer in our home office, which meant I had to plan to be on the internet. I had to plan to go to Facebook. It was ridiculously hard to post pictures of my son because I had to send them from my phone to my email on my computer and upload them! So much work!

But that year, God used the mental space to break unhealthy habits in me.

FINDING THE LIVING WATER

Social media led to a battle with a strong case of FOMO (Fear of

Missing Out). Comparison told me, "You are missing out on life" and "You are missing out on all these adventures."

Being stuck at home was not my demise. The blessing of being at home with my son was my calling. When I finally embraced the space where I was physically present, I saw God. I was not missing out. The truth was God called me to a different place in my life in that season. Different from my former coworkers and many of my social media connections and friends.

Constant social-media scrolling stirred in me a discontent with the place and space I was given to occupy. I needed to put my phone down.

In the Old Testament, the prophet Jeremiah, known as the "weeping prophet," was given a special message which finds its application in our everyday lives, too. In Jeremiah 2, he's given the proclamation from the Lord to remind the Israelites, God's chosen people, what they had with Him is what would truly satisfy them.

In biblical times, people often built their cities around rivers or lakes because water is necessary for survival. When a city would outgrow its water source, the people would make massive caverns to collect rainwater. Sounds smart, right? Spiritually, the Israelites had done the same thing. They decided their invisible God was too small. They traded authentic worship of YHWH as prescribed to them by Moses for the false gods of the people and cultures around them.

These false gods were like man-made cisterns. They looked good on the outside but had no real power to satisfy or hold water. In building their water wells, the Israelites forgot God. At its root, the fear of missing out occurs when we forget God.

Jeremiah 2:13 says, *"For my people have committed two evils: they have forsaken me, the fountain of living waters, and hewed out cisterns for themselves, broken cisterns that can hold no water."*

To forsake is to leave, desert, or neglect. Jeremiah says they forgot God, the source of Living Water, then replaced Him with cisterns unable to hold water.

Imagine their disappointment after a big rainstorm when they realized not one cistern was able to hold water. There were leaks and unseen problems below the surface. Now, there was no water and no provision for the future.

A TANK WITH NO WATER

When I was about ten years old, my parents bought two acres in the middle of my Mammaw's sprawling country land. They built a home right next to an empty water tank (think giant hole) my Papaw maintained before he passed. I have memories of him taking my cousins and me fishing there.

Before filling the tank with water, my Dad built a large wooden bridge across it. My younger sister Leyah and I had big dreams and grand plans about living next to that tank. We were talking about paddle boats, kayaks, and endless days of swimming. I could see us jumping off the bridge into the cool, refreshing water with a slight twinge of fear about what creatures lived there. (It was not uncommon to find snapping turtles or even a water snake.)

My Dad is a farmer, and his dad was a farmer, too. Being in agriculture, he was able to fill the empty tank using the farm-irrigation pipes. He hooked everything up, connecting the pipes to a nearby creek to pump water to the tank to fill it. The process lasted several days.

Finally, the tank was full. It was amazing...for a few days. Until the water drained, flooding onto the nearby field, taking all our summer dreams with it.

What happened? As years passed, gophers dug their little holes and trails all over the tank, going from inside the tank bed to the hill on the other side. The truth? This tank was not going to be able to hold any water. There was no way to pack the holes with dirt. There were just too many.

To this day, behind my parents' house is an empty tank with a bridge across it. I had real-life experience with a cistern that couldn't hold water. It was disappointing. All the plans, all the effort it took to get water in it in the first place. Gone. Much like the fear of missing out, when we replace our current callings with what we *think* would be more satisfying, we are left with nothing but empty tanks and broken plans.

ENJOY WHAT HE HAS GRACIOUSLY PROVIDED

Did you know the only place you can be with God right now is in the present? While He is omnipresent, able to be everywhere simultaneously, we – as finite humans – are not. Friend, you can experience precious joy right here. Right where you are.

The fear of missing out says:
WHAT I AM DOING NOW…
WHO I AM WITH NOW…
WHERE I AM NOW…
IS NOT IMPORTANT.

And that's exactly the mistake the Israelites made in their quest to satisfy a vertical need from horizontal sources. Because the people were not satisfied by the Living Water, they were not able to enjoy what God had graciously provided for them.

Jeremiah 2:7 says, *"And I brought you into a plentiful land to enjoy its fruits and its good things…"*

You do the same thing when you miss what's right in front of you. Not enjoying what God has given to you is a failure to fulfill His purpose. Like the Israelites, He brings you to plentiful land to enjoy its fruits and its good things. When comparison blinds you or social media leads you to envy others' possessions or experiences, you are not enjoying what He has given you! Comparison leads to unfair assumptions. It lays your everyday mundane moments next to others' highlight reels. Comparison tells you that if life were fair, things would be equal, or if you are honest, your situation would be a little better than someone else's.

Much like space and time are limited to the present, you can only please God in the present. Right where you are, you can choose to enjoy the tasks He has given you, who you are with, and where you are. Right now, you can please God by enjoying what He has graciously provided.

DENYING OUR SIN

The root of my problem with FOMO isn't my phone or social media, but the love attached to them. Money isn't the root of all evil, but the love of money is (1 Timothy 6:10). Money is amoral. When I look to money for security, control, or satisfaction, I have a problem.

We easily blame our culture for stirring this discontent or we try to shield ourselves from the world by creating a Christian subculture, which is often as sinful and idolatry-filled as the one we were trying to escape. Please don't take that shortcut and lose the endgame.

God is always concerned with where our affections lie. You are committing idolatry when you believe anything or anyone other than El Shaddai, which means All-Sufficient God, will make you happy, complete you, satisfy you, or give you peace.

A cleaner house is not going to satisfy you. A newer car will not satisfy you. Going on vacation will not satisfy you. Being tanner, stronger, or having a better hairstyle will not satisfy you. All of these are good things. They are meant by God to be enjoyed. But they are not intended to, nor can they, hold the Living Water your soul desperately seeks.

You need to stop putting up with the little voice in your head that says, *When we get to here, things will be better. When we move out of here and into this new place, things will be better. When my two-year-old is finally potty trained, then things will be great.*

That's you looking for water. And if you can be honest, waiting for the next benchmark is a well that can't hold water. It's not going to satisfy. You need to lay down your broken cisterns to embrace the Living Water.

Our hunger is too great. Our "hanger" (when we're both hungry and angry) is too strong. Our thirst is too deep to be satisfied with the temporary. These temporary accomplishments and possessions are wells incapable of holding water. Our hunger is bigger than the next job, the next pay raise, the next stage of life for our kids. We know that to be true in our heads, but we spend so much of our time striving after those things.

Jeremiah 2:35-36a says,

"you say, 'I am innocent;
*   surely his anger has turned from me.'*
Behold, I will bring you to judgment
*   for saying, 'I have not sinned.'*
How much you go about,
*   changing your way!*
You shall be put to shame."

The truth is, we are in denial about idolatry. Even as you read this, you might think the word doesn't apply to your problem.

An easy litmus test to determine if you struggle with idolatry is to look at your bank account (where you spend your money) or your schedule (where you spend your time), to find out who or what your god is.

If you are like our family and operate on a cash basis, at times, I find myself constantly checking our accounts to see what (if anything!) is in there before the next auto-payment clears. The truth is, He cannot prosper me if my confidences are in these worthless, empty wells! He loves me too much to let me deny my sin of idolatry.

Does your schedule and the way you run your day look like a clean house is more important? Or is not missing an episode of *Chicago Med* (even though you can stream it next week) feel more urgent than spending time with God? (Hand up. Guilty!)

FALSE EVIDENCE APPEARING REAL

FEAR can also be defined as False Evidence Appearing Real. When we look to cisterns that can't hold water, we look because we are fearful. This false evidence which appears real says, *She's happy, and you are not. They have it together and well, whoa, who do you think you are? You can't lead a Bible study! God is holding out on you. Life would be better if...*

If you're in a headspace like I found myself in my first postpartum season, where social media was not a healthy place, consider logging off, removing the apps, and blocking the URL. Experiment. Try something drastic, and see what God will do.

If you find yourself in a lull, where does your mind go? Where does your thought-life veer when you have a few moments to think? How good are you at waiting? Do you need to fill time? Does sitting at a stoplight mean you feel compelled to look at your phone? Does waiting in line at the grocery store mean you must check your notifications? Where does your mind linger?

These questions can help shed light on how we spend our time and resources, thus shining a light on our idols. We may be surprised to find we sought satisfying water from faulty wells.

During your battle with FOMO, please remember: God is not holding out on you.

Psalm 84:11 says,
"For the LORD God is a sun and shield; the LORD bestows favor and honor. No good thing does he withhold from those who walk uprightly."

In Luke 12:15 Jesus warns,
"Take care, and be on your guard against all covetousness,
for one's life does not consist in the abundance of his possessions."

How can we be on our guard against covetousness (which Merriam-Webster defines as being "marked by an inordinate desire for wealth or possessions or for another's possessions")?

MAKE A CHIN UP DECISION

Consider adopting one or more of the decision statements below to combat the FOMO in your life.

1. When I don't have all the facts, I will not fill in the gaps with my imagination.

This is a big one, isn't it? We can see a small snippet or hear a soundbite of someone's day or recent accomplishments and assume the worst – either about them or ourselves. Decide not to fill in the gaps. If something isn't clear or is unknown, go to the source and ask questions. Don't let your imagination tell you what's "true."

2. When I find myself feeling left out, less than, or unimportant because of comparison, I will unfollow, unfriend, or "hide" from my social media feed.

You don't need to unfriend someone; Facebook gives you options! You can unfollow a person for 30 days. If you think something is not healthy for you because you catch comparison-itis every time you scroll, it is your responsibility to remove it or remove you. If you find yourself with the spirit of discontent, put your phone down.

3. I will be intentionally present where I am by _____.

Where are you absent that God wants you to be present? Maybe you go to the backyard with the kids while your phone stays in the house, which is not far away. We all grew up as kids playing in the backyard, and our moms didn't bring their phones. Their phones were attached to the wall! And somehow, we all lived!

Being present where we are can be tricky as working moms. We live in a constant tug-of-war. I work what I call a "full-time mom and part-time, self-employed schedule." Sometimes when I'm home with my kids and have a work project weighing heavy on me, I try to be in two places at once. I rush back and forth between my two roles, as a mom and as a worker like Marvel's Flash. I rush from pacifying my littles with an entertaining yet educational television show to feverishly creating an email marketing campaign for a client on the laptop in the kitchen. When in reality, just like Flash, I'm merely creating a speed mirage – appearing to be present in one place for a moment, while I'm already somewhere else. You'll know you've reached Flash-speed-mirage status if you hear your four-year-old telling you, "Mom, look at me!" as he explains his latest HotWheels race track creation when you're in the middle of typing a report.

One of the easiest ways to embrace my present location is to write down my priorities. Instead of stopping midway through the dishes or leaving my littles in the playroom to secretly email a client, when something weighs on me, I type it in the Notes app on my phone. I have a running list of grocery items to pick up, things I want to discuss with my husband, or work items I need to get to soon. I know I won't forget the item if I make a note of it. Then I can go back to playing on the floor or taking care of my home knowing the work will still be there after the kids are in bed. My attention isn't diverted for long, and I embrace where I am and who I am with as my current God-given purpose.

4. I will instigate a plan of neglect.
(I first heard about this idea on a blog written by Ginny Washburne on mops.org).

For many of us, our phone is our alarm because we don't have real clocks anymore. And once the device is in our hands first thing in the morning, the temptation to dive right into our texts and social media is too great.

So instead of checking our social media, email, or our notifications first, assume the plan of neglect. Decide: First, I will get myself out of bed, get dressed, or have some sort of rhythm or routine before getting online. It can be as simple as planning to neglect your phone until you eat breakfast, read a chapter of the Bible, or brush your teeth.

5. I will remove these apps (_____) or make them less accessible for a season.

I didn't stay without all social media on my phone forever. After a year, I felt like I was in a good enough place to add Instagram and Facebook Messenger back. I added Facebook itself four years later. Listen to what God tells you. I did what I felt He was leading me to do. When I've realized I was adding apps back too soon, I listened to the Holy Spirit's promptings and deleted them again.

What will you regret more? Going offline and not keeping up with what others are doing or missing out on your own life?

Going four years without certain social media apps was the most healthy thing I could have done because I was in a season where I couldn't honestly say I could stay content while scrolling the lives of others.

6. I will only get on _____ if I am going to post.

Instead of getting on to scroll, tell yourself you're logging on to post. For one thing, it will make you post more! And it will get you in the healthy rhythm of not turning to social media to satisfy when you hunger for Jesus or friendship.

7. I will avoid social media on _____ (name the day/s of the week).

Maybe you pick certain days of the week to log off social media. Sunday is an easy day for me to say, "I'm not going to look at it today." I'm not going to miss much. The break is a way for me to give my mind the space to think about the Lord. As a family, we make the habit of going to church and eating lunch with my large extended family. Putting the phone down is an easy way for me to be present in these moments.

Do I do this perfectly? No. Sometimes I forget, and yes, sometimes I make exceptions for myself. But it's an attempt at rhythm and a heartfelt choice.

1 John 2:16 (NLT) says,
"For the world offers only a craving for physical pleasure and a craving

for everything we see, and pride (boasting) in our achievements and possessions. These are not from the Father, but are from the world."

This verse cut to my heart several years ago because isn't self-praise the focus on social media? We boast about our achievements and possessions. And boasting is not why we are here. If we are not pointing to El Shaddai, the All-Sufficient God, what are we doing? What's the point? How are we influencing or impacting our friends for the truth?

We can make excuses all day, and say social media is about us connecting with those far away, but if we spend hours of our precious time not enjoying what God has graciously provided, and believe false evidence which appears real, it's time to make a change and destroy some idols.

Are we going online when we are spiritually hungry? We know better than to go to the grocery store on an empty stomach, let's not go to social media with a hungry, empty heart. In both cases, we end up with what we don't need. It's best to go with a full stomach and a plan (a grocery list). I want you to go to places (social media) when you're satisfied by the Living Water and to go on purpose and with a plan. Do this because your God loves you. He knows broken cisterns like social media will not hold any water. Social media is an empty tank with a bridge over it but doesn't allow you to swim. He alone has the Living Water you need.

When you are hungry, you can choose where you look. When you are hungry, you can decide where you go. You can choose to put your phone down. You won't miss a thing.

22

PHONE DOWN
ANTICIPATE THE BLESSING

As for you, you meant evil against me, but God meant it for good, to bring it about that many people should be kept alive, as they are today. – Genesis 50:20

HAD NO IDEA HOW MUCH our boys' little Mother's Day Out program at a local church had become part of our rhythm and routine until unexpectedly, we were out of "school" for several months due to the COVID-19 pandemic. Within a week, I was unable to keep track of what day it was, and the reality that we couldn't go

23

anywhere (e.g. an indoor playground or meeting up with friends) only increased our cabin fever.

While our kids' routines were thrown for a loop, so was the intensity level at our business. What had started off to be one of our busiest years yet, turned into one of canceled events, postponed meetings, and slower client spending.

With limited groceries stocked on shelves, my beloved crunchy Facebook groups were abuzz with conspiracy theories and natural preventatives and remedies. I found myself stuck in information-gathering mode, which, if we are honest, looks more like a mom glued to her phone again.

Without my "normal" life and schedule, I had morphed into a different person, where information = salvation. Information is good. We have all seen the effects of a lack of facts. But just as crucial as having information itself is the information's source.

Does Google become my first stop when there's trouble? Am I glued to the news during a crisis? If I'm missing out on God being my go-to and find myself unable to connect with those I love the most by telling them to "shhh" because "I have to watch this," I have a problem.

FACING THE UNEXPECTED

The Bible gives us many stories about God intervening on behalf of His people who are in unexpected trouble – even if they have forgotten Him. He miraculously rescues them, and they worship Him again. Then His people are disobedient and forget about Him, and the cycle begins again.

I'd like to visit a little-known story in the Old Testament in 2 Kings 3. Elijah the prophet has been taken up to heaven in a chariot of fire; his buddy Elisha had asked him for a double portion of his spirit (2 Kings 2:9). Elijah told him, "If you see me go, then you will have it." Sure enough, Elisha witnessed the miraculous exit. In 2 Kings 2, Elisha has performed a miracle where he turned bad water good by throwing salt on it. Word gets around: Elisha can hear from the Lord. If you aren't familiar, hop onto BibleGateway.com and read 2 Kings 2 now.

Some other people you want to know from this story:

The King of Moab (Mesha, who worshipped a false god, even sacrificing his son)

Edom's King (Unnamed, perhaps because Israel, not God, appointed this leader)

Israel's King (Jehoram, the son of Ahab and Jezebel)

Judah's King (Jehoshaphat, the son of Asa, and the great-great-great-grandson of David)

King Jehoram's father dies (we'll talk more about that later), leaving his son the kingdom. During the change in leadership, the Moabites, who paid a tax to the Israelites of 100,000 lambs and the wool of 100,0000 rams, decided not to pay anymore.

Seeing the rebellion of Moab, King Jehoram decides to go after them, but he's going to need help. He gets the king of Judah, Jehoshaphat, and the King of Edom to join him on the quest. The plan is to sneak up through the desert of Edom and catch the Moabites by surprise.

There's just one problem. After only seven days in the desert, the men and animals are out of water, and things turn desperate.

SEEKING THE TRUTH

The gist of King Jehoram's first response is, "This is God. He's punishing us!" (I don't know about you, but I hear echoes of the Israelites crying to Moses in the Egyptian desert, "You brought us out here to die!")

The king of Judah says, "Don't you have a prophet of God we can talk to?" And a servant of the king of Israel says, "I know a guy. He used to wash the feet of the prophet Elijah." So off they go.

Now, remember, they didn't ask God about going after Moab first; instead, they went to their friends and neighboring countries asking for their help. Many times we do the same thing. We jump ahead and don't ask God for wisdom. I don't know how many times I have sought counsel from my girlfriends or even my Facebook friends before ever stopping to pray.

But desperate times call for desperate measures. Isn't it amazing how, when faced with situations beyond our control, we finally choose to seek the Lord?

When they get to Elisha, he tells the king of Israel, "If it weren't for the king of Judah here with you, I wouldn't even look at you." Sounds harsh, doesn't it? Remember the part where the story began, when Jehoram's dad Ahab died? Well, Elijah, the prophet, had something to do with that. He had prophesied a stern judgment on the king. Because Ahab had been so disobedient to God, Elisha told Ahab, *"You're going to die, and not only are you going to die, but the dogs are going to lick your blood!"* (1 Kings 21:19)

This prophecy becomes reality. Jehoram's dad Ahab went into war in disguise as a regular soldier, and the Scripture says in 1 Kings 22:34, *"An arrow came at random and hit Ahab between the scale of armor and the breastplate."* He bleeds to death, and dogs come to lick his blood.

We know nothing is random. God is always at work. He had been merciful to tell Ahab what was coming, merciful because it was one more way his son Jehoram would know who the True King is when the odd prophecy was fulfilled to a T.

Imagine the fear you'd feel if you're King Jehoram when Elisha says, "Go talk to your daddy's prophets – or even your mom's." His mother, Jezebel, was the one who convinced all of Israel to worship the false god Baal. Elisha pointedly asks him, "Why are you coming to me?"

WHERE TO TURN

His men are still in the desert, tired and thirsty. This attempted surprise attack on Moab, he thinks, might turn out to be how God gives them over into the hand of the Moabites for good.

We are the same way, aren't we? When things go wrong, we can be shrouded in shame and think, "This is God getting me for X." But we will see pieces of God's mercy weaved throughout this whole story. And the Bible is not simply a story about one or even a few tiny, earthly kings, but ultimately about the One True King to come.

Adverse circumstances can be used by God to show us and to convict us of sin.

According to 2 Kings 3:2-3 the king of Israel had been doing *"...evil in the sight of the Lord, though not like his father and mother, force put away the pillar of Baal that his father had made. Nevertheless, he clung to the sin of Jeroboam the son of Nebat, which he made Israel to sin; he did not depart from it."*

How do we handle a crisis? Do we avoid God? Do we immediately become convicted of sin? Do we seek God to find out what He is doing? In the passage, we can easily compare the responses of both the king of Israel and the king of Judah. After all, it was Jehoshaphat who said, "Let's find someone who knows the Lord so we can ask God."

Don't you see the mercy of God that the king of Judah is with him in the first place? Elisha speaks to the trio because the king of Judah is with them.

2 Kings 3:14 says,
"And Elisha said, "As the Lord of hosts lives, before whom I stand, were it not that I have regard for Jehoshaphat the king of Judah, I would neither look at you nor see you."

We know nothing is random – just as the arrow had found its place in the exact spot to be God's judgment on King Ahab. Nothing in our life is random, either. It's no mistake that a servant of King Jehoram knew of God's servant Elisha. It was no accident they ran out of water in the desert of Edom. It wasn't an accident when their plans failed. I could argue their predicament was part of the plan. **When the unexpected occurs, we must remember it is only unexpected to us, not to God!**

TURN UP THE MUSIC

Elisha does something interesting. He follows the statement in verse 14 with, "But bring me a musician." The scripture tells us when the musician played, the hand of the Lord came upon him. How cool is that? When he needed to hear from the Lord at a moment's notice, he quieted the noise of people's clamoring requests and listened to a song. The situation was dire, and Elisha turned on some worship music!

It reminds me of the song "See a Victory" by Elevation Worship, which has played a lot on the radio during the pandemic. It says, *"You take what the enemy meant for evil, and You turn it for good. You turn it for good."*

> If you're looking for music infused with scripture in its lyrics, check out **Rivers & Robots** on YouTube or Spotify.

Music has such power. And when we combine music that is scripture, the very Word of God – wow! The lyrics of this song echo when Joseph tells his brothers after they are reunited in Genesis 50:20,

As for you, you meant evil against me, but God meant it for good, to bring it about that many people should be kept alive, as they are today.

Later in the New Testament, we hear the evidence of the power of music to reveal God's direction in Ephesians 5:15-21 (emphasis added),

*"Look carefully then how you walk, not as unwise but as wise, making the best use of the time, because the days are evil. Therefore do not be foolish, **but understand what the will of the Lord is. …but be filled with the Spirit, addressing one another in psalms and hymns and spiritual songs, singing and making melody to the Lord with your heart,** giving thanks*

always and for everything to God the Father in the name of our Lord Jesus Christ, submitting to one another out of reverence for Christ."

There it is. When we don't know what to do, how do we understand the will of the Lord? By being filled with the Spirit (our Counselor and Comforter) and by singing truth with and to each other.

Yes, God used the situation in Jehoram's life to convict him of his sin, but He also used it for His greater purpose. There are so many layers and levels to God's movement in our lives and world.

ANTICIPATE GOD WORKING AND PREPARE FOR BLESSING

Elisha gives them some odd directions. He says, "You need to dig a valley of ditches in the desert. I know you're tired. I know you're thirsty. This whole trip is turning out to be more than you bargained for, and every moment you lose is a moment Moab might discover your secret plot. The Lord says to dig. I'm about to turn this dry streambed into water. You won't hear the storm, and you won't see it coming. I'm sending the water. Just dig."

Verse 18 even says, "This is a *light* thing in the sight of the Lord." God can easily intervene on our behalf! No matter what you face, your situation is an easy thing for our God, friends!

We need to remind ourselves and others of the truth when worry creeps up. This is *easy* for God! Our God wants to intervene on our behalf for His glory. Where do we go when we need help? How quick I am to Google my child's symptoms to diagnose their problem and start giving them what they need! How quickly I search the internet for advice about relationship disagreements, instead of first turning to the Maker of all people!

The Israelites and Edomites would have missed seeing the hand of God work on their behalf if they would have continued without seeking His help. **Putting down our phone and asking Him opens our eyes.**

During the 2020 pandemic, I saw God work in something as small as one bottle of hand soap on the grocery store shelf, which was what I needed, right when I needed it. My bathroom was out of soap. We'd been using those handy, little hotel soaps I'd saved – apparently, for such a time as this. Who knew?

How are you anticipating God working? Like the tired and thirsty men in the desert, we must follow through with obedience when He tells us what to do, even if it doesn't make sense. If God promises it, be ready. Dig the ditches. Prepare for the blessing. You can count on Him.

THE POWER OF OBEDIENCE

Prayer is powerful, and knowing we can count on God gives us immediate strength. Charles Spurgeon said, "Act not on the mere strength of what you have, but in expectation of that which you have asked."[1] We are not acting on our strength based on our current circumstances. We are acting in the strength of our Good Father.

I can only imagine the chaos that would have ensued had the men not been obedient to dig ditches in preparation for God's provision. Maybe something like a messy mudslide would have come through and destroyed any hope of them defeating Moab. Who knows? Then they would have wished they had been faithful to obey. The impossible was possible.

Thankfully, they chose to obey, even in their tiredness and desperation. The Israelites dug the ditches in the desert valley, and God sent the rain. The men and animals were saved. The next morning, the Scripture says the people of Moab woke up to something reflecting off the sunlight in the desert. They assumed it was blood! Verse 22 says, *"The kings have fought together and have struck one another down. Now then, Moab, to the spoil!"*

Imagine their surprise when it turns out to be water, not blood. The Israelites overthrow them, and it goes bad for Moab. It was what I call a "God trap." We know if they had not been faithful to prepare for the blessing, they would not have been able to receive it. The story could have gone quite differently.

A few things to remember:
   Don't accept the current state of dryness as the way it will always be.
   Don't expect the work to be glamorous or impressive.
   Don't expect everyone to understand when you obey God.
   Do expect God to move on your behalf miraculously.

You are not stuck where you are. With the power of God, anything is possible. The work was not necessarily thrilling, even though God had told them to do it! They were digging ditches! I can't imagine it being exciting work. When they were digging those holes, I'm sure at least a few of them were singing to themselves. Reminding themselves of the truth. Maybe even something similar to, "You take what the enemy meant for evil and You turn it for good."

Desperation reveals what I've been counting on, and more times than not, I count on my phone. It's a connection to the "outside world" through social media and a machine with the search engine with the answers for every question that pops into my head.

When a crisis hits, do I go inward and say, "This is God's judgment"? Do I go outward and ask my friends for their advice or help? Do I go upward like Elisha and say, "Bring in a musician. I need to hear from God" and turn on truthful music?

How are you preparing for God to move and anticipating His blessings? Consider areas of your life where you are desperate for relief, wisdom, or direction. Put down your phone. Close the laptop. Turn on some music. Open your Bible. Seek the Lord.

Fill your home with scripture and good music at the same time. Designed for families with kids, check out **Seeds of Courage** on YouTube or Spotify.

PHONE DOWN
WHAT WE NEED TO REMEMBER

But this I call to mind, and therefore I have hope: The steadfast love of the Lord never ceases; his mercies never come to an end; they are new every morning; great is your faithfulness. – Lamentations 3:21-23

WRITING HAS BEEN A BIG PART of my personal and spiritual life ever since I knew how to write. In the first grade, my friend Colleen and I came up with these wild, smiley-face characters and wrote our own story on printer paper, then stapled together to make a book. I am pretty sure my Grandma hung on to a copy or two.

Flash forward to the sixth grade when I was part of Jill Solomon's Sunday School class in our small town's First Baptist Church. As a former missionary to Brazil, her global perspective and experiences expanded our small, but growing gospel viewpoints. She passed away from cancer in 2012, but her impact on my relationship with Christ in those critical years was pivotal. Jill challenged our preteen class to realize we could experience God for ourselves. She told us to write, "I can experience God for myself" on the cover of our first class journal.

What started as writing my thoughts and prayers at the age of thirteen, continued throughout my junior high and high school years. While I was in college, journaling became the place for me to earmark the places God had brought me, to write down my prayers and a place for me to question things until He revealed the answers. Those landmark moments became the "Ebenezer," my "Thus far, the Lord has helped me" journal record (1 Samuel 7:12).

Throughout my young adult life, every New Year's Eve, I would flip through the whole year's worth of entries, reminding myself of the places God had brought me throughout the year. As I reflected on what prayers He graciously answered, I had renewed hope for the upcoming year. As I called to mind what God had done, I found hope.

UNIQUE TIMES

My fellow millennials and I have grown up in a unique time in history. Consider the advancements made as recently as the 1990s: caller ID, the internet, portable GPS, email and text messaging, Netflix, drones, flatscreen technology, Google, and DVDs. (Our kids will have no idea what it means to rewind a VHS or how to fix a cassette tape with a pencil!) Follow that up with the early 2000s with the invention of YouTube, Facebook, and the first iPhone.

Our parents had no idea who was calling them until they picked up the phone and answered! And when it came to road trips, they had to take along a giant paper roadmap and depend on a passenger to remind them of their next turn. Remember how a new edition map came out every year? If our parents had a question, they asked their parents or friends at work. They didn't have Google to ask for advice or find facts with a few taps on the keyboard. When they wanted to make dinner, they got out the recipe book; when my parents ordered takeout, they grabbed the phone book or the saved paper menu off the fridge. It's funny how quickly things change.

Some of the most Googled questions of all time (according to the search engine itself) are:

- What is my IP?
- What time is it? (If you have a device able to Google, I'm not sure why it doesn't have a clock!)
- How do I register to vote? (Look at us all being responsible citizens!)
- How do I tie a tie?
- What song is this?
- How do you lose weight?
- How many ounces are in a cup? (Yay! We're cooking.)
- When is Mother's Day? (Good for you, husbands of the world.)

Have you stopped to consider how different the world is for our children? We took more photos in my oldest son's first year of life than existed for the whole eighteen years of my childhood! And my parents were not bad documentarians! They took photos using disposable cameras we had to send to Kodak at the grocery store before we'd get prints back several days later (a few of which would be dark or fuzzy)!

In many ways, the world felt smaller during our formative years than today as we parent our children. My boys can FaceTime with their aunt, who lives states away. They often tell me what words to text to Nana, ask me to Google pictures of things, and they know how to find train videos on YouTube on our living room television.

WITH MORE POSSIBILITIES, COME MORE RESPONSIBILITIES

More than ever, we must teach our children how to handle the technology with the power to both enhance and distract from real life. But the best teachers are those who practice what they teach. The best leaders are the ones who can say, "Follow me." Do we parent by example? In 1 Corinthians 11:1, Paul says, *"Be imitators of me, as I am of Christ."* We can only expect our kids to follow God as we follow Him ourselves. Who else will show them?

A marriage ministry at our church hosts date nights for couples. You drop your kids off, go out to eat dinner at the restaurant of your choice, and return to the church for dessert and a guest speaker. Along with MOPS, this ministry drew Marcus and me to the church. You have no idea how hard it is to get a date night when you have three kids, ages four and under. ("Them's expensive," as they say.)

At one of the recent events, we heard Mandy Majors from the nonprofit organization NextTalk speak on parenting in our technology- and sex-saturated culture. I was so moved, I purchased her book, *TALK: A Practical Approach to Cyberparenting and Open Communication.*

One of the statements from her book I put to use with our young sons is, "It is your job to guard your own heart and mind." Our boys know sometimes women they see in public, television ads, or billboards aren't dressed modestly. We are teaching them that people exposing too much skin "need privacy," and it's their job to look away. We are teaching our children to take ownership of their choices.

We need the same reminder as we experience ever-changing technology and always seek to "improve" our lives. Will we manage the increased possibilities with an increased sense of responsibility?

LEARNING WHAT TO SHARE

We all know someone who shares every detail of their lives on social media – the person without a filter.

Would she be okay with her boss seeing that post?

What will her son think about how she's "venting" about him when he's grown up?

Do you need to post a selfie looking down the barrel of your blouse? Honey, I'm unfriending so-and-so for you!

We need to create a filter. Philippians 4:8 is a great place to go if we are unsure. It says, *"Finally, brothers, whatever is true, whatever is honorable, whatever is just, whatever is pure, whatever is lovely, whatever is commendable, if there is any excellence, if there is anything worthy of praise, think about these things."*

If what I am about to share online is not something that falls in these criteria, is it worth sharing? If it is not honorable, lovely, or excellent, it is not worth sharing! I have decided to avoid posting about non-gospel essential topics people like to debate. I realize not everyone has this conviction, but for me, if someone I know and love is going to get "riled up" over something, I find it's best not to share my opinion through my public social media account. I do not want to divide the house of faith (or my own family) to justify my own opinions. If the point of contention is not a black-and-white issue in scripture, it's not an issue worth debating on social media. Those conversations are better had in coffee shops or living rooms, where people can see each other eye to eye.

Some questions to ask before you post are:
- Does this distract from the gospel?
- Will I be glad I posted this later?
- Is this something I need to keep to myself?
- Is this something I can share with someone one-on-one?
- Is this honorable, just, pure, ...?

CLIMBING UP THE MOUNTAIN

In the Gospel of Mark 9:1-13, Jesus takes three of his closest disciples up a mountain. We know the story as the Mount of Transfiguration. Peter, James, and John see something they have never seen before. Verse 2 says when they got up on the high mountain by themselves, Jesus was literally *transfigured* before them.

The word used in the text is "metamorphoo" where we get the word "metamorphosis" – like the complete miraculous change in form that occurs when a caterpillar builds a cocoon and then comes out as a beautiful, winged butterfly.

Jesus, for this brief moment, stops restraining His heavenly glory. Instead, He reveals it. It wasn't light shining down on Him; it was light shining from *within* Him. Verse 3 says, *"and His clothes became intensely radiant, intensely white, as no one on earth could bleach them."*

At the same time, Elijah and Moses appear with the group and start talking to Jesus. If you're familiar with the story, you know about Peter and his lack of filter. He chimes in, "It is good that we are here, let's build three tents." The writer of Mark points out the reason he says this is because "he did not know what to say."

Don't we do the same thing? We see something amazing, we don't understand it, but we feel compelled to comment on it! We can't *not* type a response. Thank goodness for the delete comment button. I have had to use it on more than one occasion.

The truth is: They don't need tents. They are not going to stay on the mountain and have a little mini-vacation. In the midst of this, God comes and overshadows them with a cloud. They hear the voice say, "This is my beloved Son. Listen to Him." They would need this moment later in their lives. It's the same for you and me.

YOU WON'T (AND CAN'T) STAY ON THE MOUNTAIN FOREVER

Life's big moments are highlights. They are bookends. Sometimes they help us close chapters with satisfying finality, and other times they write their words on the cover of a brand-new book you can't wait to start reading. But we aren't meant to only live in the highlights. These moments of clarity and revelation are important, but we can't stay in them.

Through this story, we can also take away the truth that not everything is for us to repeat. I know how tempting this can be. If you're a nerd like me and enjoyed school and studying, then you understand the excitement that overcomes you during those lightbulb moments! You can't wait to share what you've learned. (Ask my husband how many sermonettes he's heard!) Other times, you are so deeply convinced a certain way of doing things is *the best way*, you think others will surely follow your lead as soon as your helpful information enlightens them.

But how many people have changed their political beliefs because of an article you shared on Facebook? How many memes have changed the way you discipline your child? In this polarizing culture, if we agree with what we see, we click the "like" or "share" button and move on. If we disagree, we might find ourselves getting angry or feel an increasing desire to yell at someone for their insanity. (Not you? Just me. Okay, I'm sorry.)

Sometimes, God reveals things to us for our benefit, which is what happened on the Mount of Transfiguration.

YOU'RE GOING TO NEED TO KEEP THIS TO YOURSELF

This is where a journal or private blog comes in handy. The desire to record and keep what we experienced is important. We want to look back on those moments and remember the places we went, things we did, or experiences we had. Not everything you do, eat, or place you go is a social media announcement. Not every photo is an Instagram post. (Have you seen those awkward honeymoon photos? Come on! Just stop!)

Keeping things to ourselves is also good for when we need to grapple with questions. Working through things in our spiritual walk with the Lord is healthy and a part of spiritual maturity.

From my sixth grade year on, my parents put my sister and me in a small Christian school. When I say small, I mean there were about fifty of us from kindergarten through the twelfth grade. The school itself was non-denominational, and many of the teachers came from various Christian backgrounds. Through my years there, I found different theological beliefs among my friends. Some of these were peripheral issues, but others were huge. As I tried to navigate those differences in theology, I didn't want to blindly adopt my parents' convictions as my own. I also tried to understand where my friends were coming from as they quoted scripture to back up their point of view.

In my high school years, my internet use was limited to an email account my sister and I shared with our Dad, and I don't think I considered asking Google. Without the outside sources, many of us run to first when facing questions today, I went straight to *the* source, the Bible.

God used journaling as I wrote my questions and thoughts, things I'd heard and learned. He also used scripture. I remember one question I asked Him in my prayers. Through the coming days, He brought me to the exact passages that answered my question. It was truly "the Word is alive" moment for me. I knew *why* I believed what I believed. And I knew *Who* revealed it to me. But in the beginning, I had to be okay with asking questions. I had to be okay with not knowing the answer and not rushing to other sources for answers.

Peter, James, and John had a similar experience on the mountaintop.

Mark 9:9-10 says, *"And as they were coming down the mountain, He charged them to tell no one what they had seen, until the Son of Man had risen from the dead. So they kept the matter to themselves, questioning what this rising from the dead might mean."*

These three apostles had a powerful spiritual experience, and Jesus told them not to tell the others. God is not afraid of your questions. Mountaintop experiences are worth remembering. Journals are a place for us to write those down.

YOU'LL NEED THIS LATER

You're going to need to tell others. Unlike in biblical times, we have the entirety of scripture to consult and online resources that connect us and point us to related passages. A quick search for scriptures about the transfiguration led me to one of Peter's letters to New Testament churches in Asia Minor.

Later Peter would write about his mountaintop moment in 2 Peter 1:16-18 (emphasis added),

*"For we did not follow cleverly devised myths when we made known to you the power and coming of our Lord Jesus Christ, **but we were eyewitnesses of his majesty.** For when he received honor and glory from God the Father, and the voice was borne to him by the Majestic Glory, 'This is my beloved Son, with whom I am well pleased,' **we ourselves heard this very voice borne from heaven, for we were with him on the holy mountain."***

We will need to draw from our experiences with the Lord in the future. I don't know about you, but before I married Marcus, who I would marry was the pinnacle of my prayer life! I was asking God, *Where is this man? Does he even exist?* Though I attended a wonderful Christian college with a brochure telling me a benefit of choosing a Christian college such as the University of Mary Hardin-Baylor was I *might* meet my future spouse. I remember saying, "God, if you can provide a man…" (Sure enough, God did but not in the place I initially thought. Marcus and I met my senior year at UMHB on eHarmony®.)

Or take a little over five years ago, when Marcus and I decided to expand our family. Nine months passed and nothing. I don't know how many pregnancy tests I wasted because I thought *maybe* I was pregnant. In both of those seasons of waiting and longing, God used remembering to bring me to hope.

As the writer of Lamentations says in chapter 3,
"But this I call to mind, and therefore I have hope: The steadfast love of the Lord never ceases; his mercies never come to an end; they are new every morning; great is your faithfulness."

We can be so forgetful. We are just like Peter, who suffered from doubt and denial after Jesus' arrest. Later he tells Christians in the letter bearing his name, "I was an eyewitness to this!" Peter heard God's voice. He was able to say, "I was there!" The mountaintop experience had a greater purpose.

Questions to Ask Before Sharing Online:
1. Which outlet is most appropriate for sharing this insight? Would sharing it with someone over a meal be better than sharing it with everyone on your profile?
2. Are you hoping to gain something for yourself (position, authority, the praise of others) by sharing this insight? Or are you genuinely *giving* to others when sharing?
3. Who is your audience? Is this new-found information or

experience better as a private thing between you and the Lord until you feel the Holy Spirit explicitly asking you to share it with someone?

THE DESIRE TO SHARE

The desire to share and connect with others is not a bad thing. My challenge is to make sure you use the right venue to share. Not every outlet is an appropriate outlet. Not every prayer request needs to be shared with your eight hundred friends online.

The challenge is finding those select, trustworthy friends with whom to share those intimate, authentic moments. Peter, James, and John no doubt talked to each other about their mountaintop experience and their questions about what Jesus meant by rising from the dead. Who had ever heard of such a thing?

I found a trustworthy friend in my college roommate Jessica (chosen "at random" for me my freshman year by the university). Before moving in together in 2007, we only shared our names and dorm room colors – what priorities!

And a funny story – Jessica first thought I would be African-American because my name "Kennan" is often mistaken for "Keenan." While I imagined she would be a super tall, burly girl because I knew she was playing basketball for our university women's team. Neither was true. She was shorter than me, and I am a pasty white girl, a shade 02 Vanilla, according to Bare Minerals.

Our friendship grew over our God-arranged living arrangements. Jessica is still someone I can call or text with those deep, intimate prayer requests or life moments. Anytime my family drives through

Waco, where she and her family live, we always stop and stay. She is one of a few friends I can pick back up right where I left off, no matter how much time has passed. We can process things together, share our doubts, and authentically celebrate when we see God's answers on our behalf.

LOOKING BACK

While the Mount of Transfiguration wasn't about journaling, it was about God revealing Himself to those who would become world changers. These were people who would make the dominoes fall leading to your salvation experience and mine. Take a moment to look back. Where has God brought you? In what ways has He grown your faith? What do you call to mind to lead you to hope?

> If you're looking for an excellent resource for how to study the Bible, check out **Jen Wilkin's** *Women of the Word.*

When looking at scripture, ask things like: What did this mean in its original context? What does this say about God? Then end with: what is my response to this? How does it apply to my life?

PHONE DOWN
WE ARE HIS WORKMANSHIP

For we are his workmanship, created in Christ Jesus for good works, which God prepared beforehand, that we should walk in them. – Ephesians 2:10

THINGS ARE ALMOST NEVER AS EASY as they seem. Growing in our walk with the Lord, learning a new skill, or renovating a house is not as easy or as fast as it looks on TV. We live in the age of HGTV where home renovations take less than an hour and are full of laughter and end with the perfectly decorated homes of

49

our dreams. In our first house, Marcus and I embarked on a weekend project of adding small tiles to the wall behind the mirror in our guest bathroom. Though it was a mere six-foot by three-foot space in need of tiling, we almost killed each other that weekend. The project lasted way longer than it should have, and we got super frustrated with each other. We can laugh about it now, but back then, we seriously wanted to hurt each other.

Despite the warning we should've heeded from our first mini-reno experience, we dove headfirst into the world of home renovation when we purchased our second house in need of rehab five years later. It was the perfect location for us, six houses away from my grandparents, a few from my aunt, and another few from my uncle and his family.

Our house needed love. The carpet was full of cat hair. The bathrooms were outdated and the kitchen boasted the super-popular brown panel cabinets from the 1960s. I'd like to tell you my husband and I are super carpenters, but in reality, we were the visionaries of this whole project. Papaw, my Dad and my uncle were the muscle. We demo-ed the entire house, replaced flooring, painted walls, and lost a hall closet to enlarge the tiny master bath.

Why am I telling you all of this? Because unlike your favorite episode of *Fixer Upper* in which Joanna calls the future homeowners about an unexpected expense, and they reply with a half-hearted not super surprised, "I guess we have to do it," we had a few surprises of our own. The cameras weren't rolling, and there was no design budget we could "borrow" from for the unexpected expenses.

When we wanted to replace the flooring, we found asbestos tiles, and because of the danger of the material, we needed to call in an abatement team, which cost money. We were so disappointed. And though the other, less expensive and much-advised option was to add the new tile on top of the old tiles (leaving the asbestos alone), we both didn't feel comfortable with that idea.

Maybe it was the surprise problem or maybe it was the young mama bear in me picturing my second-born learning to crawl on the floor with *cancer* under it, but we paid the abatement team to come in. They wore full HAZMAT suits and removed it. I can remember seeing the bare concrete throughout the house and being so glad for the fresh start. The surprise slowed us down, but it wasn't going to steal our enthusiasm. There were more surprises ahead, and we ended up living with my parents for three months, but the end result was worth it.

Friend, the surprise asbestos and the not-to-code plumbing were not a surprise for God. And God is not surprised by the work that needs to be done on and in us. He is not surprised by the things in me that are "not to code." He knows I am finite and remembers I am dust (Psalm 103:14). God knows what He's doing when He chooses to begin a good work in us. Friend, it's always been about His capacity and not our own.

FACING YOUR FEARS WITH FIRE

Sometimes we are our own worst enemy. We talk to ourselves with language and a tone we would never accept coming from another human being. Have you ever thought about that? Even if you consider yourself an introvert, you talk to yourself more than you talk to anyone else. Jim Jensen, the author of *7 KEYS To Unlock Your Full Potential* said, "We talk to ourselves all day long at the rate of 150 to 300 words per minute."[1] That's a whole lot of self-talk.

We spend an average of five hours a day on our phone. So it's not a stretch to say what we look at and engage with on our devices plays a large part in framing our self-talk. We talk to ourselves in a way we would never speak to anyone else.

Look at her! She's so put together. Her hair is always perfect, and she dresses so stylishly. Your hair is so stringy and thin.

Oh my goodness! She grows her own carrots! And they're organic. And her kids actually like eating them! You have rotting produce in your refrigerator.

Oh, look! They went with friends to the zoo. They got their faces painted and everything. You never get to go on playdates. You haven't been anywhere in weeks. You don't have any real friends.

Do you see how unfair that is? Do you see how quickly scrolling for a few minutes in your "me time" has turned into listening to an undercurrent of an unhealthy and very untrue narrative? The truth is – you *do* look cute in your favorite pair of mom shorts. You did so well eating salad for lunch three times last week, although picking the *giant* tub of organic greens at the grocery store was a little ambitious. You *do* get to go places and meet up with friends, but your littles aren't interested in posing for pictures with big smiles while on the merry-go-round yet. You are a beautiful person with immeasurable value because you were created by God. You are not missing out simply because your life and opportunities do not mirror social media. You mean so much to many many people. You matter.

Friend, your self-disqualifying has to stop. You are not the one in charge. You are not the one who decides who is disqualified. God does. And He says, *I choose you. I wove you together in your mom's womb whether she expected her pregnancy, was planning on it, longing for it or not. God says, I was not surprised when you entered the world. I planned you. I picked that day. Your quirks. Your talents. Your fears. I know them all.*

When we face our fears, God replaces them with fires that can't be put out. Another way to think about this fire is that God gives you something you can't *not* do.

Mandy Arioto the founder and CEO of MOPS said, "Some women fear the fire, some women tend their God-given fire and use it to light up their hearts and their world. Let's be those women."

Marcus and I had a fire-we-couldn't-put-out experience almost three years ago when we started our business. If you told me we would be self-employed even five years ago, I would not have believed you.

When we started our family, we were both working at jobs we enjoyed *immensely.* He was working as media director at our church creating videos, handling the website, and doing graphic design. We had built many wonderful and deep friendships there. I was working as lead associate editor at a magazine with lots of fun people. I literally loved going to work every day. Even during our stressful deadline-heavy seasons, I relished it. I can still picture myself in my business casual getting to work early enough to head over to the nearby Starbucks for an iced caramel macchiato. I am so thankful for the years I had there.

EMBRACING THE CALLING

When we first moved to my small hometown of Devine to be near family after spending our first seven years of marriage in the Houston area, I was in culture shock. I had been a stay-at-home mom for about two years, doing freelance writing and editing on the side when it came along. Marcus was working as a sales rep for a company offering media and tech equipment for churches. We both knew it wasn't his forever-job. We were desperate to find some sense of God's calling. We were at an all-time financial low, and this time we had two kids in the mix.

God was gracious to us even in that. We found ourselves more willing to take risks because we literally had nothing to lose. We both felt like we couldn't *not* try working for ourselves. We made the leap, telling our network of friends and family, "We're doing this full-time now!" We used a spare bedroom as our office and stepped out in faith. Every single month God was faithful. We saw business pick up steadily and met new people in our surrounding communities, but God kept on pushing us.

Back then, our boys required a car ride to get them to go down for their afternoon naps. We'd pack up the CR-V and drive around our small town talking as they dozed off to sleep. We felt that fire again. This time, we felt convinced we needed commercial space. We needed to get our business out of the house. While it was "fun" (and I say that with quotation marks on purpose) to have potential clients over to our dining room while my toddler boys roamed around, we were outgrowing it. I had dreams of hosting creative workshops and classes and had even had success when my childhood friend Hilary taught hand-lettering (you guessed it) at my dining room table.

All this dreaming led to lots of prayer, lots of searching until we found the commercial space we rent now. We celebrate two years here in 2020, and I'm amazed at how God's prompting kept pushing us along the path to something bigger than we would have thought was possible on our own.

God ordained work for *you* to do.

Have you thought about this truth lately? It was easier to dream about who we would become or what we would do while we were teens or in college. *What's the "thing" I'm going to do?* We may have focused on a certain career path or a title like nurse, teacher, or lawyer.

As a new college grad, I vented to my friend Crystal because I worked in a job not suited to my personality. She had taken a nannying gig while she took graduate courses. She encouraged me to keep pushing to find something I would enjoy. Though I *felt* stuck, I needed to be reminded that didn't mean I *was* stuck.

We need to unravel the myth that limits the words "good works" in Ephesians 2:10 to mean we will have made it once we have a particular role or title. Just as I didn't reach the end of where God would have me when I made it to the editor job I loved, He is not done with me even now. Marcus and I may not be self-employed our entire careers. God is always building us and preparing us for what's next. Don't limit yourself to a particular title or singular role for your entire life. There are infinite facets to God, and there are different times and seasons for each of the roles He will use you throughout your life.

IT'S MORE THAN A TITLE

We know good works are not only about what we do or our unique skills. Our God-given calling is more than our occupation. Many of us millennials have already had *many* occupations. And as my fellow stay-at-home/work-from-home moms can tell you, on average, we've worked for four or five bosses before we quit to become our own boss.

Henry Blackaby says in the Christian classic *Experiencing God*, "God is always at work around you."² Look where He is working and seek to join Him. The book of Acts tells us He's determined the boundary of our dwelling places (Acts 17:26), which applies to the boundaries of our influence, roles, and responsibilities, too.

God invites us to join Him and gives us purpose. He never says our identity is determined by our productivity or our own goodness and morality.

Ephesians 2:4-7 says (emphasis added),
*"But God, being rich in mercy, because of the great love with which he loved us, **even when** we were dead in our trespasses, made us alive together with Christ —by grace you have been saved – and raised us up with him and seated us with him in the heavenly places in Christ Jesus, so that in the coming ages he might show the immeasurable riches of his grace in kindness toward us in Christ Jesus."*

Because of Jesus, God will never stop relating to you on the basis of grace.

Ephesians says He loved us *even when* we were dead in our trespasses and sins. His love is not based on how well you're doing right now. His love is not based on whether or not you've lost your temper with your kids in the last week. Sometimes I feel like I have one of those construction site signs above my head that reads, "Temper-free for ten days." Then I lose my cool and ruin it. The sign flips back to "Zero temper-free days." And I'm left to try harder to have a better attitude.

Knowing His love and His purpose are not based on how well I am doing is so refreshing and life-giving. His choosing of us and our value was placed on us *before we* were called His workmanship. I love how He ordains the scriptures in perfect order. He didn't put verse 10 before verses 4 and 5.

Ephesians 2:4-5 and 10 say,
"But God, being rich in mercy, because of the great love with which he loved us, even when we were dead in our trespasses, made us alive together with Christ – by grace you have been saved ... For we are his workmanship, created in Christ Jesus for good works, which God prepared beforehand, that we should walk in them."

Now that I have my order right – my identity and value are set first – then I am equipped to use my gifts and to do the good works He has planned. I should not keep this grace and calling to do good works to myself. If it all stops with me, I become a cesspool. I was designed to be a river. His goodness and grace flow through me. If you listen to the voices of comparison and fear, you can turn into a puddle, not a life-giving stream. If you turn into a five-hours-a-day social media consumer as you endlessly scroll, you miss out on the opportunity to be a life-giver like Jesus, and that's the ultimate good work.

THE BANNER OF GRACE

So how do we go about doing this good work? We choose to live under the banner of God's grace. Think of it as resting in the hammock of God's grace because we put all our weight on Him. We stop working to earn, and we work because of what He earned for us on the cross. I would add, grace isn't a hammock to fall asleep in. Though rest is a part of our weekly Sabbath routine, grace is also used by God to propel us into action. As blogger Laura Singleton put it, "Grace isn't a hammock to nap in until we die. Grace is a slingshot to the abundant, adventurous, dependent life God has for us."[3]

If we're not living under the banner of grace, we miss out on abundant life. We can start believing lies without looking at life through the lens of truth. We believe the lie that we must earn God's approval.

When we don't live under the banner of grace, we move toward people-pleasing. When we don't live under the banner of grace, we can wrongly say "yes" to every opportunity instead of seeking God's will. When we don't live under the banner of grace, we can respond to life in anger when things don't go as planned – as if God owes *us*. When we are not living under the banner of grace, we can respond in anger to those around us, like when your husband doesn't foresee your plan for the day, even though it was all in your head. *(You mean, he's not a mind reader yet?)*. When you are not living under the banner of grace, it can lead you to apathy. This is especially dangerous. This mindset is where you don't care about your relationship with God. You don't take the time to connect with Him. You switch on the Christian autopilot and handle things on your own, not allowing Him to transform you into the likeness of Christ through your everyday circumstances and the study of His Word.

YOUR VALUE IS GIVEN

The truth is our value is given to us. It's not determined by the work we do. "You are God's workmanship," Ephesians says. But what does this mean? The Jerusalem Bible translates it as His "work of art" or His "beautiful poem."

You are no longer named "daughter of disobedience" as we were described earlier in the chapter. Instead, you are called "daughter of grace." Because of that, we are not controlled by the passions of our flesh. We are clothed with supernatural power to operate differently.

We are walking in life. We have a big-picture view. Eternity is set on our hearts (Ecclesiastes 3:11).

Understanding our God-given value equips us to rightly use our gifts for Him.

Where do you create beauty in your world? Where do you come alive? What activities make you feel energized? What makes you think, *Wow! Did God give me this gift?*

Do you ever wonder, *Am I doing this for myself? Is that selfish? Will they think I'm doing it to get attention?* Sometimes the mere fact that we are asking those kinds of questions is proof we are not in it for the limelight or the attention it will get us and proves we are walking in God's calling. You have the choice to let fear win or trust God and what He called you to do. Obedience doesn't make you an instant expert. It's OK to be a beginner. Trust God to guide you through the process. Take one faith step at a time.

Write first, edit later is a concept that applies to our gifts and one I learned from Sean Wes, an accomplished podcaster and course creator. My claim to fame with Wes :) is when Marcus and I sat behind him at a conference for creatives in Dallas in 2015. We remember him because of his distinctly long hair and the fact he was from San Antonio (I am from the small town of Devine, which is thirty miles south of SA). I thought to myself, *One day, my husband and he are going to be besties. It's going to happen.* LOL.

Wes says when writers try to combine writing and editing into one process, we get stuck. We try to write and edit at the same time in our heads so what comes out on the keyboard is the "right" thing to say.

We take too long to think and thus, we take too much time to write and from too filtered a space.

We can pre-filter our gifts, too. If you have the ability to sing and love to sing, and your church allows people to perform "special music," as they called it in my childhood Southern Baptist church, then why in the world are you not singing a special every now and then? You may have trapped yourself, by editing, thinking, *I must practice this song more before I can go up there to sing. I don't have time to practice because I have a toddler and a baby, therefore, I'm not going to be singing in church until ten years from now.*

This line of thinking may be extreme, but you get the point. The why-not-now? concept was beautifully asked and addressed by another one of my faves, Amy Jo Martin, who hosts the "Why Not Now?" podcast and was a guest at Christy Wright's 2018 Business Boutique conference.

Too many of us don't walk in our gifting and calling because we're too busy editing ourselves first. When we should write first and let it be a mess. Let there be spelling mistakes. Let there be the wrong "their" there. For goodness sake, if we all waited until we could do things exactly right before we went public, would there be any entertainers? Or musicians? Or creators of beauty in the whole wide world?

THERE IS ROOM FOR YOU

We also believe the lie that someone else is already doing what we'd like to do and doing it better than we could, so therefore, there is no room for us.

The world has room for you and room for your gift. People you know, who are in your sphere of influence, will respond to you.

This truth is in the Bible, friend. Ephesians 2:10 says, "There are things God has prepared for *you* to do." Quit disqualifying yourself before you even start by comparing yourself to others you want to be like. Shut down the app, get off the phone, and go do something yourself!

God placed people in your sphere who are not in my sphere! People know you, trust you, and like you, and they don't have a clue who Sean Wes even is! And if God is infinite, infinitely creative, and made *you* to do specific good in your world, then He is creative enough to not make a duplicate. He is creative enough to equip you in a new, unique way that will please Him and bring Him honor and glory.

Life is not about you, but you are invited to be His beautiful work of art. We are given this unique opportunity, in this unique time in history, with these unique technological advancements and outlets so we can be image-bearers of our great Creator. People need your gift. People need to see the reflection of a Creator who loves them in your life and through your service.

LIKE MOTHER, LIKE DAUGHTER

You may have heard the sentiment that whatever we want our daughter to think about herself and her self image, we need practice in front of her, which has led to a lot of moms proudly wearing bikinis (I don't know about that part. LOL). But this adage is a true principle for sharing our gifts.

If we want to show our daughters what it means to use our gifts for the Lord without comparing ourselves to others, then we must show them. I mean, I got the benefit of going through junior high before smartphones! Praise Jesus! I graduated high school before VSCO girls or TikTok or ____ fill in the blank for whatever is popular right now.

Without the foundation of truth to stand on, to tell us how to handle the responsibilities of having a smartphone – with more processing power and memory than the earliest desktop computers – we could miss out.

When I prepare to meet my family's needs beforehand like my boys' lunches and their little backpacks with "homework" inside their cute folders, I am doing it out of love. I anticipate their needs and make sure, by golly, juice boxes and their favorite flavor of LÄRABAR® are plentiful.

Sweet friends, God has prepared things *in advance* for you to be part of. In His grace and mercy, He equipped you with everything you need. You have Him.

You are not like the children of wrath, like the rest of mankind (Ephesians 2:3). You have a new identity. I want to close this chapter with a paraphrase of the passage we've been digging into. If this passage is something you've heard a million times, sometimes reading a different translation can bring you new and fresh eyes.

A paraphrase of Ephesians 2 in *The Message* says,
"It wasn't so long ago that you were mired in that old stagnant life of sin. You let the world, which doesn't know the first thing about living, tell you how to live. You filled your lungs with polluted unbelief and then exhaled disobedience. We all did it, all of us doing what we felt like doing, when

we felt like doing it, all of us in the same boat. It's a wonder God didn't lose his temper and do away with the whole lot of us. Instead, immense in mercy and with an incredible love, he embraced us. He took our sin-dead lives and made us alive in Christ. He did all this on his own, with no help from us! Then he picked us up and set us down in highest heaven in company with Jesus, our Messiah.

Now God has us where he wants us, with all the time in this world and the next to shower grace and kindness upon us in Christ Jesus. Saving is all his idea and all his work. All we do is trust him enough to let him do it. It's God's gift from start to finish! We don't play the major role. If we did, we'd probably go around bragging that we'd done the whole thing! No, we neither make nor save ourselves. God does both the making and saving. He creates each of us by Christ Jesus to join him in the work he does, the good work he has gotten ready for us to do, work we had better be doing."

KENNAN BUCKNER

5

EYES OPEN

BUILDING YOUR GOD-CONFIDENCE

And the Lord said to him, "But I will be with you..." – Judges 6:16a

IN MY EARLY TWENTIES I was a smartphone holdout. I did not want to have the ability to get on the internet wherever I was. I was fine paying a dime per text because it meant I didn't message people very often and wasn't included in every family group-text.

Fast forward a few years, I'm now on my second iPhone and a mom with a couple of kids when a new message appeared on my screen after a software update:

Congratulations, your iPhone usage is down 33% from last week.

I thought to myself, *Sweet! I didn't even realize I was looking at my phone less this week. Look at me doing good.*

Then it read:

For an average of 3.1 hours a day.

Three hours a day?! Y'all. I could not believe it. This busy working-from-home mom didn't even have time to paint her own toenails, plan ahead for weekly meals, or remember to change the air filters in my house, yet somehow I averaged three hours a day on my phone! It didn't seem real.

The little notification punched me in the gut because I thought I was doing much better than I was. My eyes opened to the truth. When was the last time I spent *even close* to that amount of time with the Lord on a given day?

My eyes-open truth was: I have the time. My phone was an idol.

ADMITTING THE TRUTH

I confess to you as I did to my fellow MOPS moms in a devotional shortly after that moment: I had the time. I was choosing how to spend it. My phone was winning.

Remember what we said about how we spend our time and money shows us who our god is? I had made an idol out of my phone. There's no other way to cut it. If I can give three hours a day to my phone and another two to my favorite television shows, then maybe my problem isn't that I'm using technology, but the *way* I am choosing to use it.

I am not using those devices to connect to the truth. Instead of watching another episode of *Dateline* (I mean, shocking. Someone dies, and big surprise, someone did it), how about I watch an inspiring Bible teacher? Instead of scrolling and scrolling, growing more and more discontent with the way I've decorated my house or how disorganized my pantry and laundry rooms are, what if I filled that time on my phone with, I don't know, reading the Bible, listening to audiobooks or scripture put to music?

And there are so many good Christian podcasts to play in your earbuds. I could learn about parenting, deepening relationships, or strengthening my marriage because of the wide range of topics. The Christian community produces much better content that is so much less cheesy than it was during our parents' early days.

THE CYCLE OF IDOLATRY

So how did it get this bad? How did I slip into this idolatry? Well, it's not unlike how it happened in biblical times. Let's go to the book of Judges to a story about Gideon.

Judges is a history book in the Old Testament outlining the judges and leaders of the tribes of Israel before they became a kingdom. All of its stories follow a cyclical pattern: there's God's blessing, followed by complacency from His people, followed by sin, which leads to suffering (usually at the hand of their enemies), followed by a cry for

KENNAN BUCKNER

help and repentance, and ending with God's deliverance and blessing. The cycle repeats throughout the entire Old Testament. I'm convinced it repeats in our hearts and lives as well.

In our story, a man named Gideon is threshing wheat in a winepress, which is a chore done on a hilltop so the wind can carry off the chaff as the wheat falls down into the pile. This isn't the method Gideon uses. He's threshing wheat in the secret of a dark pit of the winepress because every time the Israelites thresh wheat, the Midianites and Amalekites come to steal it. It wasn't only their wheat, they stole everything they had.

Judges 6:4 says,
"They would encamp against them and devour the produce of the land, as far as Gaza, and leave no sustenance in Israel and no sheep or ox or donkey."

They would come "like locusts" (vs. 5) and eat everything. I have the feeling it's not unlike when your house is clean, the refrigerator is fully stocked, no crumbs litter the floor, and your kitchen sink is empty. Then your family comes back inside from the backyard and like a whirlwind – shoes and socks fly, snacks are had, and the cycle starts anew.

The people's response to this outright bullying was to cry to God for help. God sends a prophet who tells the people, "Look, I delivered you from the Egyptians, and I have given you what you needed. But you haven't obeyed Me. I told you not to fear their gods because I am your God." God in His mercy uses the oppression of the Midianites to draw His people back to Himself.

A DIVINE EXPERIENCE

We're told the angel of the Lord visits Gideon while he's threshing wheat in the winepress with an important message: God is with you, mighty man of valor.

Mighty man? he must have thought. *I'm hiding away doing menial chores.* What I love about Gideon is his fearlessness in asking questions. The people are in dire straits, and it seems like God has left them to fend for themselves. They've heard stories from their parents about the Israelites' miraculous exit from slavery in Egypt. But those stories seem like just that. Stories. Let's listen in on their conversation.

Gideon's Question #1:
If the Lord is with us, why has all this happened to us?

If I am honest there have been times in my life when I've asked this question: Like when mom's breast cancer returned forcing her to do more chemo, even after she'd undergone double mastectomy. Or when a friendship that used to be so strong suddenly fizzled and faded. Or when my husband felt he couldn't give his all at work anymore, and we weren't sure where we would go next.

Why has all this happened to us?

Before he takes a breath, Gideon asks another question of his heavenly visitor.

Gideon's Question #2:
Where are all His wonders our fathers told us about?

Where are all the miracles our parents say God did for them? Has God stopped intervening? Is He not aware of what is happening to us these past seven years? Does He even care about us?

God was at work around Gideon, even during this time. Let's keep reading.

ANSWERING OUR OWN QUESTIONS

We are so much like Gideon. We sometimes answer our own question before we are quiet long enough to let God speak. Gideon answers his own doubts and fears with this (vs. 13): *"But now the Lord has forsaken us and has given us into the hand of Midian."*

I know why all this has happened: God abandoned us.

I want you to hear a heavenly honking horn and see red lights flashing. NOT TRUE. Friend, no matter what you are going through God has not abandoned you, and He did not abandon Gideon and the Israelites either.

I have compassion for their situation. I can easily talk back to Gideon, "You should trust God" because I know the rest of the story. I have the privilege of seeing the Bible already written. Gideon was living this in real-time.

The Midianites oppressed the Israelites for seven years. They had suffered long. Their sense of normalcy had been ripped from them for almost a decade. They were miserable. They cried out to God, "Why are you letting this happen to us?" God reminded them, "I am the One who gave you this land. I am your God. Don't worship their gods. But you have not *listened* to me."

Do we take time to listen to God? Do we ask our questions and wait for His answer? So often we falsely equate bad things happening in our lives to God's abandonment, which is not the truth, but a lie from the enemy.

The angel of the Lord answers Gideon in verse 14, *"Go in this might of yours and save Israel from the hand of Midian."*

The angel of the Lord tells Gideon he is going to be used to save Israel from the hand of Midian. That's good news, right? Let's see what our friend Gideon says.

Gideon's Question #3:
But Lord, how can *I* save Israel?

How can you ask *me* to do this for You? Don't we ask God the same question? We are so quick to disqualify ourselves so we don't take the step of faith required for obedience.

We need to stop trying to build our own self-confidence, and instead work on building our God-confidence.

I'm not qualified. Don't you know my family? Haven't you seen how much I blow it with my kids? I am such a failure in _____ (name the area of your life where you constantly struggle). *I am not friendly enough. Outgoing enough. Prepared enough. I've never been to seminary.* And on and on our excuses roll.

Friend, you are significant. You have a God-given purpose. You may think you need certain qualifications, but God is the One who qualifies. We need to stop trying to build our own self-confidence with likes,

71

shares, and comments of approval, and instead work on building our God-confidence.

I love God's simple reply. Verse 16 says, *"I will be with you."*

ASKING FOR A SIGN

Gideon asks for confirmation that this is a word from the Lord. He asks the angel of the Lord to wait while he goes to prepare a young goat and unleavened cakes. Gideon cooks for him. The angel tells him to put the prepared meal on a rock; Gideon obeys. Then the angel touches the tip of the meat with his staff and fire springs up from the rock and consumes it all. Then the angel of the Lord disappears!

In his fear, Gideon says, "Oh no, I've seen the angel of the Lord face to face." When he experienced the holy, the weight of his own unworthiness made him afraid. Just as darkness is chased away by the light, when holiness gets near us, it dispels the darkness in us. It can't survive.

God assures him with this (vs. 23): *"Peace to you. Do not fear; you shall not die."*

Think of that! Peace. Do not be afraid. You are not going to die. You will survive this in-person meeting with My presence and what's coming next, a battle with the Midianites.

The Lord revealed the aspect of His **peace** right before He was sending him to **war**. This new revelation of God's character was what Gideon needed to know before being sent to battle. God gives us exactly what we need. Gideon built an altar and named it, "The Lord is Peace" in response to this truth.

FACING THE TRUTH

Throughout my thirty years on the planet, God has shown me an aspect of His character right when I needed it. He is infinite in knowledge, friends. Every corner of our mind where we stash worry, every Plan B we create in case God doesn't come through, and every to-do list we draft, points to who we count on: *ourselves.*

I'm convinced He often allows situations beyond my control to remind me I was never in control to begin with. It's a realignment, and in this realignment, I can fight it and make it more painful on my part or I can choose to submit, to point my mind and heart in the direction He is pushing and let Him move.

God is so faithful to send me an unexpected text or letter in the mail through a friend, the little nudge to remind me it was God talking to me, calling me to obedience. Even as I was preparing this chapter, I thought, *God is this really a theme here? Or am I trying to turn all these unrelated pieces into a book because I've always wanted to write a book? Am I forcing this? Will it even make sense?* Then in the same breath, as I am listening to recordings from devotionals I shared with our MOPS group on kennanbuckner.podbean.com, I hear the words, "God opened my eyes." Y'all that was the theme for this section of chapters before I even reviewed this lesson. It gave me such a sweet sense of His direction and provision. Just as He says to Gideon, He says to you, "I will be with you. Peace to you."

DESTROY YOUR IDOLS

The same night, the Lord speaks to Gideon again and gives him another piece of the puzzle. Before he's to deliver his people from the Midianites with the Lord's help, he has to do something very, very hard, and not too popular. Verses 25-26 say,

"Take your father's bull, and the second bull seven years old, and pull down the altar of Baal that you father has, and cut down the Asherah that is beside it and build an altar to the Lord your God on top of the stronghold here, with stones laid in due order. Then take the second bull and offer it as burnt offering with the wood of the Asherah that you shall cut down."

God tells Gideon to remove the family's idols and to destroy them. The private encounter with the Lord isn't enough. He now has to make a public statement. It's not going to be popular or received well, but this step is the right thing to do. So Gideon grabs ten friends to help him, and they destroy the idols in the middle of the night.

Word gets out the next morning when the people wake up to see their god destroyed. They find out it was Gideon and want to kill him. His father Joash basically says, "If Baal is mad about it and he's a real god, then Baal can take care of Gideon himself." So the people go with that. They give Gideon the nickname Jerubbaal, meaning "Let Baal contend against him."

In the following chapter in Judges, we see how God – in a miraculous way – frees them from the Midianites. But friend, if those idols had still been up, who do you think would have gotten the praise? The Israelites would have credited their relief from the oppressive Midianites to those false gods. The One True God was not going to let that happen.

We cannot expect the presence and peace of God to go with us into battle if we refuse to remove the idols in our lives.

I may not have a statue in my house, or bow or pray in the name of other gods, but I do have idols.

A song written by Ross King and made popular by musician Jimmy Needham says,
"Anything I put before my God is an idol
Anything I want with all my heart is an idol
Anything I can't stop thinking of is an idol
Anything that I give all my love is an idol"[1]

What do you need to tear down so you can experience God's victory?

TRUTHS TO REMEMBER

Maybe to experience victory, first we give up the idols in our life so God gets all the credit when those victories come.

The odds are impossible or as I like to call them "God-sized" for a reason. Judges 7 is a more well-known part of the story. God has Gideon slim down the army to a mere three hundred men. What was he going to do with three hundred men? Win a battle.

Asking God questions is okay. Gideon shows us it's okay to ask God, "Is that *really* You?" if we are asking in purity of heart and readiness to respond in obedience. Gideon is included in the long list of faithful followers known in the "Hall of Faith" chapter in Hebrews 11.

WHAT IS HE ASKING YOU?

In all of Gideon's questions, the Lord then asks *him* a question. And it's not too big of a stretch to say God asks us the same thing. Verse 14 in the NIV says, "Am I not sending *you*?" (emphasis added)

Gideon hid threshing wheat. God calls him a mighty man of valor. Gideon asks questions. He's open about his failures and his past. God says, "You are someone I can use."

Where is God sending *you*? Is there an aspect of His character He has revealed to you for no other purpose than it is what you will need for your next step? He reveals Himself as peace right before Gideon goes to war. Gideon is faithful to destroy the false gods his family and community worshipped.

Something big was ahead, and he would give God the credit. Gideon knew *who* was responsible for the victory, and he wasn't going to obey only in the cover of night anymore.

What I find amazing is a few verses later after their vicotry, the people are ready to make Gideon their king. He's done something no one else could do. After years of oppression, the people are free! But Gideon replies with such wisdom in Judges 8:23,

"I will nor rule over you, and my son will not rule over you; the Lord will rule over you."

Just as we were reminded earlier in the story that Gideon's family had told him the stories of God's faithfulness from their slavery in Egypt, we are reminded to verbalize the mission and work of God when we see Him at work around us. We must point out the traces of His hand in real-time to those God places in our path. We want God to get the credit for His work in our lives, rather than the idols those around us may worship.

When we are faithful to obey Him and give Him the credit for the victory, we become builders of God-confidence. God desires that our own eyes be open to the idols standing in the way, blocking us from experiencing victory. He alone is God. He invites us to be part of His purpose by sharing the truth, helping to open the eyes of those around us. That is the mission of God.

EYES OPEN

DO NOT HARDEN YOUR HEART

For He is our God, and we are the people of His pasture,
and the sheep of His hand. Today if you hear His voice,
do not harden your hearts... – Psalm 95:7-8a

N COLLEGE, I VISITED A NURSING HOME with my friend Sarah. She committed to spend time at the same nursing home weekly to talk with strangers, which terrified me.

On one of those trips, it struck me how some of the older people we visited were gems: so sweet and such a refreshing presence. The kind of people you leave and think, *I want to be like her when I am old*. Then the stark contrast is right down the hall with someone who is angry, fussy, suspicious, and easily offended. There it was, an easy comparison, a soft heart versus a hardened heart.

Which one will you be? A singular choice or decision doesn't lead to the final result. One choice or event doesn't turn them into hard-as-a-rock people. The same is true for those who leave us feeling refreshed and encouraged. Being interested in the lives of others and putting others before ourselves is not a one-and-done decision. (Wouldn't it be so easy if it were?)

I thought about some people I know personally. Who decides who is going to end up crotchety and who will be sweet even as their memories fade and their strength and eyesight wane? I know who I want to be like. I want to have a tender, soft heart when I am old, which starts with having a Christ-like heart today in my seemingly small, day-in and day-out choices.

DAILY DECISIONS

I can harden my heart in small ways every day. I harden my heart when I let circumstances grate on me, bother me, anger me, or turn me inward instead of letting Christ refine me.

We know love keeps no record of wrongs and covers an offense, yet I somehow justify hardening my heart when I don't serve my little people with gladness, but become frustrated when they need my help getting something from the pantry again! In those moments, I need to remind myself, blessed are those who even give a cup of water to one of these little ones in His name (Matthew 10:42).

I harden my heart when I don't treat my husband as a partner and a teammate, but as an opponent who needs to be outscored. I need to remind myself love keeps no record of wrongs, and it is patient and kind (1 Corinthians 13:4-8).

I harden my heart when I don't soften toward my people in the small, routine activities and chores, like when I am too focused on the task at hand to respond to them with my full attention, especially ironic is the same task which was so "important," I will later call demeaning and belittling. I need to remind myself God calls me to love others as Jesus loved me and gave Himself up for me (John 15:12 and Ephesians 5:2).

IDENTIFYING THE SYMPTOMS

We have identified some of the symptoms of a hardened heart as described by David in Psalm 95, a short song of eleven verses, so please take a moment to read it. We can see more from God's heart if we step into *where* David was when he penned those wonderful words under the influence of the Holy Spirit.

He was probably out in a field because he was still a shepherd. Many commentators believe David was in his teens or early twenties when he wrote Psalm 95. This psalm was written *before* he was king of Israel, likely around BC 1015. Five years prior to this, David was (secretly and surprisingly) anointed king by the prophet Samuel. But the fulfillment of God's promise had not yet come. Soon after, David the shepherd boy is a lyre player and armor bearer for King Saul. Scripture says when a harmful spirit from God came upon Saul, David would play and Saul would be refreshed, and the spirit would leave him (1 Samuel 16).

We are told by Samuel when David is anointed king, the Holy Spirit rests on him from that day forward. He is under the leadership of the Holy Spirit and yet, here he is, still a servant. **God placed David in service and in proximity to leadership of Israel for a reason.** I wonder as I read Psalm 95 if this was one of the very songs David sang to King Saul during his distress.

I wonder as David the shepherd boy's words and music echoed down through the palace halls who heard the song:

"For He is our God,
and we are the people of His pasture,
and the sheep of his hand.
Today, if you hear His voice,
do not harden your hearts, as at
Meribah,
as on the day at Massah in the wilderness,
when your fathers put Me to the test
and put Me to the proof, though they
had seen My work."

What is David talking about? To find out, let's go back to Exodus 16 and 17. The Israelites have just escaped from the hands of the Egyptians. God gave them bread from heaven called "manna," which literally means "What is it?" God established the Sabbath as a day of rest, and people start to quarrel about the lack of water.

Exodus 16:4 says (emphasis added),
"Behold I am about to rain bread from heaven for you, and the people shall go out and gather a day's portion every day that I may test them whether they will walk in My law or not."

God was seeking their belief, obedience, and trust. It was a *daily* obedience because they were told to gather the manna they needed for each day, except for Fridays. On Fridays, they would gather a double portion to last them through Sabbath. They experienced the day-to-day miracle of the Lord because every person had exactly what they needed. The passage tells us if anyone tried to hoard more than they needed, it would spoil and stink.

Despite this hand-to-mouth miraculous way of life in the desert, the people continued to question and quarrel – as David described in Psalm 95 – they hardened their hearts. We see an example of one of those questions in Exodus 17:3 which says,
"Why did you bring us up out of Egypt, to kill us and our children and our livestock with thirst?"

They question the very motive and intention of God. They question His purpose for them. Not in an inquisitive, "God, we want to know your purpose for us" type of way, but in a fist-in-the-air, "How dare you bring us here?" type of way.

Because of this, verse 7 continues,
"And he (Moses) called the name of the place Massah and Meribah, because of the quarreling of the people of Israel, and because they tested the Lord by saying, 'Is the Lord among us or not?'"

The names Moses chose have significance. The name Massah, means "testing" and Meribah means, "quarreling." The scripture tells us why

Moses did this. It was because they tested the Lord by saying, **"Is the Lord among us or not?"**

Like the Israelites in this story, I have a hard heart when I experience unrighteous anger or when I am *unrightfully* angry. I have a hard heart if I try to live on yesterday's bread so I don't need to come back to God *every day*. Instead of getting my daily bread from Him, I reveal to my Good Shepherd by my actions that I doubt His goodness. I doubt His character. Just like the Israelites wandering for 40 years, I doubt His presence in my life and wonder, *Is He with me or not?*

TREATING THE DISEASE

How do we combat this pervasive disease of doubt which leads to a hard heart? The antidote is found right there in the Word.

Know He is the Lord your God (Exodus 16:12)
God has a proven track record with you. From the Middle Eastern disciples who first shared the gospel of the risen Savior around the world all the way to the person who introduced you to God, He marked the path for you. He is not only the God of your grandparents and parents, but *your* God when you put your faith in His Son Jesus.

Keep this as a testimony (Exodus 16:31-36)
The Lord commands Moses to keep a jar of manna for future generations as a testimony of His provision for them in the desert. And wouldn't you know it, the jar did not spoil or get stinky. What do we need to keep as a testimony of God's provision? Maybe you're an artist and you can paint a picture to remind you of His love, or you're like me and you just *know* an artist. My cousin Dusty is an amazing artist and graphic designer and I shared with him a personal story of

God's provision. I didn't tell him what to paint. I only shared the story and told him whatever it stirred up in him, to paint it for my living room wall. His painting is one of my most treasured possessions, a reminder for me, a talking piece when guests enter our home, and a teaching moment for our children.

Ask for what you need and know He is with you (Exodus 17:1-7)
We can expect God to continue miraculously providing. He did not bring the Israelites out in the desert to kill them. God promised Abraham that all the nations of the earth would be blessed through him because the longed-for Messiah would come through him.

When the people ran out of water, they went to Moses to complain, "God must have brought us out here to make us die of thirst." Moses went to the Lord and asked for what the people needed. God tells him to strike the rock with his staff, and He will provide water from inside a rock. Moses used the same staff to strike the Red Sea and it parted, allowing the Israelites to pass through on dry ground, escaping death at the hands of the Egyptians. Visual pictures. More miracles. More evidence of God's presence. God was not finished with His people, and He is not finished with you.

EYES-OPEN TRUTH

Do I allow the circumstances of life to refine me to make me more like Christ or do I harden my heart? When I come up short, am I quick to complain or to ask God for what I need? **God calls us to live with daily dependence on Him.** He wants us to come to Him every day for what we need. David recognized this. As a shepherd himself, he knew God was more than worthy of praise and worship for being our Maker, but He is worthy because He is a Good Shepherd who leads us every day into the safe pasture we need. His rod and staff comfort us (Psalm 23); He protects us from harm and guides us. Are our hearts soft to His gentle leading?

I harden my heart when I feel a small tug of the Holy Spirit to turn off the screen (whatever device it is) and seek true rest for my soul in the pages of His Word, but choose to ignore His whisper. As moms, we can get caught up living for bedtime. I live to get through the day so I can make it to bedtime, then I can watch what I want to watch and eat whatever I want without having to share! Don't get me wrong: some days we do need time to ourselves. (No guilt trips here.) But if I am feeling a heavenly tug and choose to ignore it then that's a "today" I have chosen to harden my heart and to ignore my Shepherd.

...do not harden your hearts, as at Meribah, as on the day at Massah in the wilderness, when your fathers put me to the test and put me to the proof though they had seen my work. (Psalm 95:8-9)

The Israelites may have thought spending forty years going in circles was a waste of time. David may have wondered why, after being anointed king, he was still an armor bearer and harp player. Nothing is wasted by our God.

There's a Jason Grey song called "Nothing Is Wasted" which says:
"The hurt that broke your heart
And left you trembling in the dark
Feeling lost and alone
Will tell you hope's a lie
But what if every tear you cry
Will seed the ground where joy will grow

And nothing is wasted

Nothing is wasted
In the hands of our Redeemer
Nothing is wasted

It's from the deepest wounds
That beauty finds a place to bloom
And you will see before the end
That every broken piece is
Gathered in the heart of Jesus
And what's lost will be found again

Nothing is wasted
Nothing is wasted
In the hands of our Redeemer
Nothing is wasted"[1]

In the amazing, all-powerful hands of our Redeemer, not a thing is wasted. Remember w*hose* you are and let this truth inform your everyday decisions to soften your heart to His leading.

KENNAN BUCKNER

7

EYES OPEN
REMEMBERING WHOSE WE ARE

The thief comes only to steal and kill and destroy.
I came that they may have life and have it abundantly. – John 10:10

ABOUT A YEAR INTO MARRIAGE, Marcus and I adopted a puppy from the local animal shelter. The day we went to the shelter we saw all kinds of dogs. We knew we would pick a small breed since we were living in a one-bedroom, eight-hundred-square-foot apartment at the time. Passing up the Chihuahuas that had my eye,

Marcus was instantly drawn to this little Rat Terrier whose tag read "Darwin" (terrible name for a girl dog by the way). The description on her cage said she had arrived at the shelter the day we came.

We sat in one of the shelter's visitation rooms to meet her and hold her. She was so nervous and cute. And that was that. We renamed her Reba, after you guessed it, Reba McEntire. (My college roommate got me addicted to the show *Reba*. Marcus was baptized into it because I registered for the entire series of six seasons on our wedding registry. Thanks again, Renda in Arkansas).

Reba is the best puppy. She loves crunching ice cubes and going on walks around the complex. We potty trained her more easily than we'd later potty train our humans. On our walks, she even picks up plastic bottles people leave behind and carries them home, earning her the name "little recycler."

A few years later, the three of us moved into our first home. She has a yard and a bedroom to herself. She was living it up. One morning after

Marcus left for work, Reba ran out the front door. Reba had escaped before, and it was no big deal. Marcus and I would chase her down, corner her, and end her little escapade of fun.

This time, with a newborn in my arms, I could not chase her. I panicked. I thought, *She's little. She's cute. She's gone. Someone is going to ignore her collar and dog tag and take her. We'll never see her again!* Immediately, I went to our subdivision's Facebook group and posted her picture asking people to please keep an eye out for her.

Then a neighbor suggested I put out some of our dirty laundry on the front porch so Reba would *smell* us. She would smell where she belonged and come back home. I thought it was worth a try! And I had plenty of dirty laundry. So I filled up a basket and stuck it on the front porch.

About thirty minutes later, I heard Reba at the front door. She'd come back! It was such a relief. I was like, *"Thank you, God. You even care about our animals!"* Fun fact about dogs, did you know they can smell forty times better than humans? This sense of belonging to the Buckners brought Reba back to her home where her toys, stash of cleverly-hidden bones, and her people were.

KNOWING WE BELONG

We were created to connect and belong. And when we get off course, we may not smell our way home by catching whiffs of dirty laundry on the wind, but we *can* find our way back. Our Good Shepherd leaves the ninety-nine to find us.

Throughout scripture, God calls His people His sheep. "Sheep" provides a sense of belonging, like Reba has with us. God is the One who provides for us, keeps us safe, brings us into His pasture. Our whole life is dependent upon Him, just as Reba would have no idea where her food or water comes from apart from the dog-food bucket and the faucet.

This brings to mind a familiar verse in John 10:10. You may know it by heart, but I'm going to include it here anyway. Try to take it one word at a time.

"The thief comes only to steal and kill and destroy. I came that they may have life and have it abundantly." John 10:10

The Word is so rich and full! More than a Hobby Lobby poster for your wall or a shareable artsy phrase for your social media profile. The context of this verse is so important. In the previous chapter, we see Jesus is talking to a crowd of Pharisees when He tells this story about sheep. He healed a blind man on the Sabbath. A big no-no because you weren't allowed to do any work on the Sabbath. (Remember how we saw in 2 Kings when Elisha says this is a *"light"* thing for God? This is one more way He shows us it is not *work* for Him to bless His own).

Even the Pharisees were confused by Jesus' actions because the man, born blind, could now see. He didn't lose his sight in a freak accident or develop an illness where loss of sight was a side effect; he *never* had vision. The people believed if you had a physical ailment such as blindness, it was the result of either your sins or your parents' sins. Jesus debunks this poor theology in John 9:3 which says,

"Jesus answered, 'It was not that this man sinned, or his parents, but that the works of God might be displayed in him.'"

No human on earth who could give this blind man the healing he so desperately needed. Nothing like this had ever happened before. The religious leaders weren't sure how to categorize Jesus. John 9:16 says,

"Some of the Pharisees said, 'This man is not from God, for he does not keep the Sabbath.' But others said, 'How can a man who is a sinner do such signs?' And there was a division among them."

The blind man's parents are called in because these Pharisees want confirmation that the man was born blind and is their son. His parents acknowledge that yes, this is their son, but how he was healed, they will not repeat their son's account of the events. They don't want to be kicked out of worship by the Pharisees. They care more about their own skin and reputation than that of their son. (Verse 22 says the Jews had already agreed that anyone who confessed Jesus as the Christ would be put out of the synagogue).

So the Pharisees, still trying to get to the bottom of this mystery, call the man again and get him to say, "If this man were not from God, he could do nothing," which to them is the same thing as saying Jesus is the Messiah, so they kick him out of the temple. The healed man is an anomaly. He's ruining their peaceful, quiet Sabbath where people follow their rules and follow *them*.

Jesus was going to do more than rock the boat, break their rules, and ruin their popularity contest. He was here to lay down His life for His sheep. His sheep would hear His voice and follow Him.

WHO DO YOU LISTEN TO?

Being a sheep who follows the Good Shepherd is not just about who you *belong* to, it's about who you *listen* to. What is the direction of your listening in day-to-day life? In John 10, Jesus points out several areas of listening that get us into trouble.

Sheep have a cool hearing ability. They can direct their ears to the sound they want to hear. Their ears capture a wider frequency of sound than is audible to human ears. Because of this, when the shepherd approaches his sheep, he uses a soft, reassuring tone of voice, letting his sheep know he doesn't mean any harm. His voice is familiar to them because they hear it often.

Just as sheep have the decision of where to turn their ears, we turn our ears. Are we listening to the Good Shepherd? We must use our ability to turn our ears to the voice we know because this is vital to both the quality of our life and life itself.

OTHER VOICES

As Jesus talks to the Pharisees who have kicked the blind man out of their synagogue, he points to three others His sheep may look to for life.

The Stranger
"A stranger they will not follow, but they will free from him, for they do not know the voice of strangers." John 10:5

The voice of the stranger is something that conjures up thoughts of elementary school "stranger danger" and some cartoon-style villain ready to snatch up unsuspecting children by baiting them with candy or lost puppies. What we see in scripture is that familiarity with the Good Shepherd's voice becomes the litmus test for safe versus unsafe people. The voice of the stranger causes alarm in His sheep because it doesn't sound like the well-known voice of their Good Shepherd.

I would challenge us to realize the areas of our lives where we have listened to the voice of strangers over the voice of God. An easy example of this in real life is not everything labeled "Christian" or "religious" is true. I don't know how many memes with quotes attributed to "strangers" I have seen shared or posted by friends who do not speak the truth! Oftentimes, all it takes is a quick Google search to see how the person does not stand up for the truth in the whole of scripture.

> If you want to learn more about this, check out the films *American Gospel: Christ Alone* and *American Gospel: Christ Crucified*.

Not everything wearing the label "Christian" is theologically correct. What is theology? The study of the nature of God. So *not everything* in the Christian section at your favorite bookstore tells you the truth about God. It's time we, the sheep, develop discerning ears so we recognize when something is off.

The Bible is the basis for what is true about God and what is false. Many people have fallen for the stranger's voice who offers an "all roads lead to God" theology. But friend, can I be honest with you? Jesus didn't teach this. The sentiment is blatantly false.

A. W. Tozer said, **"What comes into our minds when we think about God is the most important thing about us."**[1] We must get this right. Religious divisions are a part of the fabric of history. Even some of the

Pharisees in Jesus' day thought He broke the Sabbath by healing the blind man while others thought He was from God to perform such a miracle. Even among the Jews, the chosen people of God, there was division. Division does not scare us away from Christ. It calls us to caution. We can't take every "Christian" thought at face value. We take the words of others and compare them to the voice of the Good Shepherd.

The Hired Hand

"He flees because he is a hired hand and cares nothing for the sheep."
John 10:13

This warning from Jesus reminds us of the hired hand, someone who is paid to dependably care for the sheep. You may have people in your life who *should* care for you, and they don't. You may have experienced wounds because of the hired hands in your life.

It always struck me that the blind man's parents did not stand up for him when they were interrogated by the Jewish leaders. When the Pharisees called them in to ask them about their son, they were passive. In essence, they said, "Go ask him!" because they didn't want to be kicked out of the temple. You would think their excitement for the son's new-found sight would overshadow their self-protection or that the weight of the miracle would outweigh their desire to protect their own ego.

Hired hands exist in our lives, too: people who have the God-given responsibility to be our provider and to tend to our care, but do not protect us from the wolves. Instead, when danger comes, they flee.
My challenge to you is to be open with your Good Shepherd about those wounds. Sheep are highly tolerant of pain. Sometimes they will hide their pain so they won't look like the weakest link in the herd,

leaving themselves open as the first target for predators. Friend, we also hide our wounds and our pain. We don't want to be seen as the weak one in the crowd. Jesus contrasts the uncaring hired hand with Himself, all-caring and all-loving.

No other human can be your Good Shepherd. Only Jesus. My husband is a godly man, but he cannot be my Good Shepherd. Others throughout our lives, maybe parents or relatives, fell short in their roles of protectors or caretakers. They fled when they were supposed to stay. They didn't defend us like they should have. Hear Jesus again say in John 10:11,

"I am the Good Shepherd. The Good Shepherd lays down His life for the sheep."

The Thief
"Truly, truly, I say to you, he who does not enter the sheepfold by the door but climbs in by another way, that man is a thief and a robber." John 10:1

Jesus also points out the thief is someone who "climbs in by another way." Anyone coming in by another way than the door (Jesus) Himself.

In my first job out of college, I worked at a Christian bookstore on the southside of Houston. As I came in one Saturday, I rounded the corner into the staff break room and met a big, burly man. A robber. In our split second interaction, I didn't have much time to think or even become afraid, I said, "Excuse me?"

He quickly said he must have gotten turned around looking for the bathroom. I knew this wasn't true. But I wasn't the police, I was in "keep us all safe" mode. So I led him back through the door clearly marked "Employees Only" and showed him to the restrooms.

The man was a thief. He came in to steal and got away with some cash from my fellow assistant managers' purse. She'd been to the bank before her shift, and the man had likely been watching her.

He had ulterior motives for being in the store that day. He came for the purpose of stealing. As I reflect on that experience, I am grateful to the Lord for His protection over me. I am glad no one was hurt, and the thief only got away with a few bucks.

Jesus said anyone who does not believe that He is the doorway is a *thief*. Anytime we try to enter by our works or what we are *not* doing, we are missing the door. We are trying to climb in another way. Salvation is not about good outweighing the bad, because it's not about us.

Jesus says in John 10:9, *"I am the door. If anyone enters by me, he will be saved and will go in and out and find pasture."*

Are you walking through the door? Are you listening to the Good Shepherd? Is He leading you in and out to find good pasture?

I shared before how social media became a thief in my young adult life. It robbed me of my joy, my peace, my contentment, my vision, my mission. Just like the maxim which says you become who you hang out with, I became riled up when I saw Facebook friends turning confrontational. In the wake of national tragedy, if people posted about death, politics and suicide, I found my own spirits low. You don't want to put an invisible shield around yourself to block your compassion receptors, but you do need to be in a soul-safe place before entering the world of social media.

On her Instagram account, author and speaker Kelly Needham talked about her temptation to work or do house chores before spending time in the Word. Throughout her walk with Christ, she found seeking to have her soul in order *before* her house in order kept her on the right track. She would repeat to herself "soul in order before house in order."

We all experience the longing for external things to be *just right* before we sit down with our Bible and meet with the Lord, don't we? We want the dishwasher empty, the kids asleep for a nap or off at school, and the laundry finished, folded, and put away. We value external order more than the internal order which comes from spending time with our Good Shepherd.

But friend, in order to *recognize* the stranger's voice, we must first *know* the Good Shepherd's voice. Those in the banking industry recognize legitimate currency by spending hours studying the real thing, so when a fake bill crosses their path, they immediately know it isn't right.

THE ABUNDANT LIFE

The abundant life we seek won't come by listening to strangers. It won't come from the hired hand and certainly won't come from the thief. The satisfying, abundant, more-than-enough life we seek comes when we follow our Good Shepherd to find good pasture.

The truth is: Our daily life cannot be abundant if our ears are tuned to the voice of strangers. Our daily life cannot be abundant if we are looking to the hired hands for provision. Our daily life cannot be abundant without walking through the door of Jesus.

The Good Shepherd came in the flesh over 2,020 years ago. He came to bring life and life abundant. Jesus laid down his life for us. We forget what His sacrifice cost Him. He left the glory of Heaven, confined eternal God-sized glory into a human body, and submitted Himself to death on the cross.

He reminds us, *I've given you special sheep ears so you get to choose where you turn your ears.* And for the places where hired hands have let us down and let wolves into our lives, He reminds us of *whose* we are. We belong to Him. He brings us back into His care, and where thieves have come in and robbed our peace and our joy – He reminds us He is the door and any self-dependence or other-dependence we have is worthless. He speaks to us, we know His voice, and He makes us sheep who follow Him.

EYES OPEN

THIS IS THE DAY THE LORD HAS MADE

This is the day the Lord has made,
we will rejoice and be glad in it. – Psalm 118:24

IF YOU GREW UP A TRUE SOUTHERN BAPTIST GIRL, you probably went to G.A. (Girls in Action) camp for five glorious days in the summer. If you're from Texas, you and I may have even floated on the Frio River together and didn't even know it. I attended G.A. camp every summer from the third through sixth grades. Some of my best friendships grew strong there. Our camp counselors were volunteers from our church, including my childhood friends Hilary, Sarah, and Janie's moms. They woke us up in the mornings with their exuberantly clapping as they sang,

"This is the day, this is the day,
that the Lord has made, that the Lord has made,
I will rejoice, I will rejoice
And be glad in it."

It was annoying and fun all at once, and it accomplished its purpose. We woke up excited for another day of adventures at Alto Frio Baptist Camp. To this day, every time I read Psalm 118:24, I remember those summer camp mornings.

The psalm is everywhere, right? On thousands of Instagram memes with beautiful flowers and mountain views behind it. On hand-lettered anything. This verse is the ubiquitous pep talk for our spirits when we're feeling blue.

But I want us to go deeper than that. Psalm 118:24 is so much more than a "you should feel good about today" pat on the back. This verse is deeply misused and misunderstood. We use it to beat ourselves up when we think we should feel better about our current situation no matter how hard it may be. We can use it to try to conjure up some sort of spiritual feelings, or to stir up a contentment we aren't experiencing in the present moment. Friend, we don't need to fake joy. We don't have to deny our reality. We *can* rejoice because this news is so good. Hang tight.

REJOICING IN...

We do not merely rejoice for another day of life, though life is precious and we should be glad because every day is a gift from God. This is rejoicing on a *specific* day. It says, "*This* is the day..."

So what day are we talking about here? Let's read the passage in its context. This psalm was assumed to have been written by David. It was penned after the northern and southern kingdoms of Israel were reunited. Jesus would later quote this psalm to the chief priests and Pharisees after they ask by what authority He taught and performed miracles (Matthew 21).

(This portion of the psalm begins with a word picture – the "gates of righteousness," which bring to mind the door and the gate we talked about in John 10.)

The context of this familiar verse is Psalm 118:19-24:

"Open to me the gates of righteousness,
  that I may enter through them
  and give thanks to the Lord.
This is the gate of the Lord;
  the righteous shall enter through it.
I thank you that you have answered me
  and have become my salvation.
The stone that the builders rejected
  has become the cornerstone.
This is the Lord's doing;
  it is marvelous in our eyes.
This is the day that the Lord has made;
  let us rejoice and be glad in it."

The gate of righteousness David foresaw is the gate of Jesus Christ. He is also described as the stone, the chosen one or cornerstone. Who are the builders? They are the ones who reject the chosen stone. In this case, the Jewish leaders who reject Jesus as God's chosen cornerstone are the builders. Remember, this psalm is written years before Jesus walked the earth as a man, so it is both a prophecy and a promise.

Peter also talks about the cornerstone when he tells the Jewish leaders the whole gospel story in Acts 4. This takes place after Jesus' death and resurrection, and the boldness in which Peter and John speak astonishes the religious leaders.

Peter tells them in Acts 4:11-12, *"This Jesus is the stone that was rejected by you, the builders, which has become the cornerstone. And there is salvation in no one else, for there is no other name under heaven given among men by which we must be saved."*

The cornerstone is the first stone laid when building a structure. Everything laid after it will be set in reference to this chief stone. The cornerstone determines the position of the entire structure. Friend, if we don't put Jesus first, as the first stone we lay our lives upon, we're going to be cattywampus. He is the only foundation for salvation. No one can be saved except by His name.

"For no one can lay a foundation other than that which is laid, which is Jesus Christ." 1 Corinthians 3:11

THIS IS THE DAY

So what *day* are we rejoicing in? We are rejoicing in the day God made the rejected stone the cornerstone. The author isn't writing about being happy today regardless of your circumstances. He is talking about *this* day. This chosen, specific, planned-in-advance miraculous day Jesus Christ was chosen by God to become the cornerstone, the very foundation of our faith and the righteous gate through which we, sinners, can enter and be saved!

Jesus also calls Himself the stone. In Matthew 21, He tells the story of the vineyard owner who sends his servants to the tenants to collect his fruit, and instead the tenants choose to mistreat the servants. So the owner decides to send his son, saying, "They'll respect my son." And instead the tenants think to themselves, "This is the heir. Let's kill him."

Jesus follows this story by quoting our psalm in Matthew 21:42,

"Jesus said to them, 'Have you never read the Scriptures?:
The stone that the builders rejected
has become the cornerstone;
this was the Lord's doing,
and it is marvelous in our eyes?'"

To tell the chief priests and scribes, "Haven't you read this before?" was undoubtedly offensive to them. Of course they had read it before. The Jewish leaders were very knowledgeable and had spent hours and hours since their childhoods memorizing the Torah (the first five books of the Bible).

Jesus adds that anyone who falls on the stone will be broken to pieces, and the stone crushes anyone it falls on. Jesus warns that all their head knowledge was not softening their hearts to the truth. **The stone they rejected would one day crush them because they refused to look at it and be crushed by their sin recognizing their need for a Savior.**

Are we broken by what He has done for us? Or will He break us because of our rejection of Him? The truth is God sent Jesus to the vineyard to collect those who are His.

THE MASTER'S PLAN

When we take "this is the day the Lord has made, let us rejoice and be glad in it" and try to stick it on this present day, we miss it. The day we rejoice in is the day God's chosen stone was made the cornerstone. **God's plan before you were even born was to call you to Himself and rescue you.** That. Is. Amazing. That is a day we can rejoice and be glad in.

So when we put on today the burden of the promise in Psalm 118:24, we're not in the right day. We have the date wrong. We must go back in time to the day when the very Son of God died for us on the cross and three days later defeated death when he rose from the grave. The day He became the cornerstone is indeed rejoice-worthy.

Don't Christian-ese every experience into a social media post and miss the richness of the context of scripture. If I'm being honest, this past week, our kids have been nuts. They've stopped napping. Week four of self-quarantine for COVID-19 has us driving each other crazy. Parts of our day are rough and not very rejoice-worthy. Our perspective on life is all about what/who we are looking at. Are our eyes open to the truth? Are we looking to the cornerstone?

UNPERMITTED ADDITION

I enjoy the HGTV show *Flip or Flop*. The California couple (now separated) bought run-down dumps and turned them into beautiful, high-dollar properties. Like many married couples, they disagreed when it came to major decisions. Tarek always wanted to be cheap. He would usually pick the beige and tan, and the most plain styles for tile and paint colors. While Christina was always pushing the limits of their budget and going big for the high-end finishes.

My Dad is similar to Tarek. He is a factory-model, keep it beige, "Why would you want a bright color?" type of guy. (Total side note/funny story: When I was growing up, my Dad went on a fishing trip with his buddies, and Mom decided it was time for new carpets and fresh paint. She let me – a five-year-old – pick my bedroom colors. I chose to paint my room hot pink and the carpet was green. Can you imagine? I don't know what I was thinking, but I liked it!)

God love 'em, Tarek and Christina were always running into unpermitted additions. Making renovations on a home and keeping additional rooms without the inspector's permission is against California state law. The structure may appear to be sound or have been built well, but it doesn't matter. If the original construction didn't have the proper paperwork or plans in place, Tarek was legally required to tear it down.

Do we have unpermitted additions? Do we have habits and routines that don't belong? That are not permitted? Friend, we must tear those down. They are not part of God's original plan.

The building is angled on the cornerstone. This stone gives perspective to everything else. Jesus gives perspective to everything else in our lives: how we treat our spouse and children, how we handle our money, the boundaries for how we handle our phones and devices, the effort and integrity we bring to our jobs.

We cannot rejoice with unpermitted additions in our lives. We can't tack on whatever we want to the foundation of Jesus Christ the cornerstone. We can't add rules-based living which ignores grace and an intimate relationship with the chief stone. We can't ignore God's moral code and live according to the passions and lusts of the flesh.

A DAY TO REJOICE

What *day* is marvelous in our eyes? What is the day we are glad and rejoice in? The day Jesus saved us! We cannot water down the verse to a pep talk we give ourselves when life is legitimately difficult. We don't have to do that. Go back to verse 21 which says,

"I thank You that You have answered me, and (You) have become my salvation."

When I put the weight of that promise on *today* and I miss the context of the promise, I force myself into a fakeness which is not healthy or helpful. If my portrayal of life every day is a day I rejoice in, then I must provide the context for rejoicing for it to benefit anyone who may be watching on their Facebook feed. The context is Jesus.

Am I saying we must air our problems on social media? Share pictures of our dirty sinks and disorganized rooms in the name of being authentic? No. But I do believe we are called to share our lives in the context of the cornerstone upon which our life is built.

9 FEET READY
OUR PRINCE OF PEACE

For He Himself is our peace, who has made us both one and has broken down in His flesh the dividing wall of hostility. – Ephesians 2:14

CONSIDER MYSELF A FAN OF THE SAN ANTONIO SPURS. I remember the late 1990s and the days of David Robinson and Avery Johnson. I even met Johnson in the fifth grade when he came to my elementary school. I've attended a handful of games, and every time I have so much fun. I drink way too much Coke and root for my team who always seems to struggle in the fourth quarter. Fast forward to our days living in Houston, where the only team broadcast on antenna television was the Houston Rockets. Sad day.

On a recent date night, I took Marcus to a Spurs game after we'd moved back to San Antonio. We did one of the fabulous Park & Ride options from Blue Star in Southtown, where you eat dinner at a restaurant then they take you to and from the game. You don't pay for parking, and they pick you up right outside the gate when the game is over. Dinner and tickets were an expensive date night for us. I remember our evening, not only because we went to a NBA game or spent big money, but because we enjoyed being together.

For the first time in a while, we didn't have the loudness of life and the demands of parenting small children. All we had was a menu of delicious choices, the cool evening, a good game, and an almost carefreeness about us. We talked "shop" about what was going on in our business, but we also talked about our hopes and dreams. How one day, we'd come to another Spurs game and go all out: sit in front-level seats and buy the $10 sweet tea and maybe even stay in a downtown hotel instead of going home after the game.

Deep, dreaming conversations with our spouses may not be accessible in the everyday grind of life. Work, children, and responsibilities seem to take all our time and energy. Now, I'm no marriage expert, but I can see the small moments of focused time together as necessary for the health and growth of our relationship.

The same is true of our relationship with God. We cannot expect to grow deeper in our spiritual walks without times of uninterrupted, focus and attention, spent together.

Many of us, unfortunately, maybe don't *long* for time with God or notice when it's missing from our lives because we have a skewed view of who He is and what He wants from us.

Once when I was watching the Spurs play the Rockets on television while we lived in Houston, the referees called a foul. The Rockets drew the foul, and it looked gnarly. Of course the benefit of television is seeing the instant replay. In my "professional" opinion, it was obvious this guy from the Rockets was acting. I know the Spurs have been accused of "flopping," too, but this was unbelievable. The replay was unnecessary.

We do the same thing to ourselves. When we blow something, we see the instant replay in our own heads. We may see ourselves, others, or even God wearing the referee uniform blowing the whistle at us. Calling foul. Our mess-ups and mistakes play over and over and over.

You weren't fully present. You spent the whole conversation scrolling on your phone.

You lost your temper. Can you imagine what so-and-so would say if they saw you talking to your kids with that tone?

You messed up again. You get all worked up over stuff that doesn't even matter.

You're such a failure. Could God even use you?

Friends, we don't need to live in guilt because the Prince of Peace came to our rescue. Our sins don't have dominating power over us anymore. Sure, we will probably still experience the natural effects of our sin, but God is not trying to pick a punishment for when we blow it. He isn't throwing the Law out, either.

In a shocking display of godheaded justice and love, He both fulfills His own demands, and at the same time, rescues us in spite of our inability to keep them.

THE PRINCE OF PEACE

Chances are, you're familiar with the often quoted "Christmas-card" verse in Isaiah 9:6 which says,

"For to us a child is born,
to us a son is given;
and the government shall be upon his shoulder,
and his name shall be called
Wonderful Counselor, Mighty God,
Everlasting Father, Prince of Peace."

Have you ever stopped to think about what the title Prince of Peace means? The Book of Isaiah is the one place this name for God is used in the entire Bible. We also get a glimpse of this Prince of Peace in the book of Ephesians.

Paul wrote the letter to the church in Ephesus, a city he visited on his second missionary journey. He stayed there for two years ministering and teaching. These people knew Paul. They loved him. He wrote Ephesians while in prison for his faith to encourage them. In the first half of the letter, he reminds the early Church about big, theological truths. In the second half of the letter, he speaks to how their lives are changed as a result of those truths.

In Ephesians 2, Paul talks about Jesus being our peace. He reminds them salvation was not only for the Jewish people, but all along, God planned to bring in the Gentiles (everyone else including me) into His sheepfold. Ephesians 2:14-16 says (emphasis added),

*"For He Himself is our peace, who has made us both one and has broken down in His flesh the **dividing wall of hostility** by abolishing the law of commandments expressed in ordinances, that he might create in himself one new man in place of the two, so making peace, and might reconcile us both to God in one body through the cross, thereby killing the hostility."*

What is the dividing wall? Other translations call it the "barrier" or the "middle wall of separation." To find out what it is, let's go to the Old Testament after the Israelites have escaped Pharaoh, and God gives Moses instructions on how to build the temple.

Now remember, much of the Old Testament is also giving us pictures or "shadows" of the things to come. They are true in their present time, but they also represent bigger truths. These parallels are God's way of helping us understand, much like the parables Jesus used to help the disciples wrap their head around big, chunky truths.

In Exodus, God tells Moses to build the temple with three main sections: (1) an outer court where common everyday Israelites could go, (2) the Holy Place where the Levites and priests could go, and (3) the Most Holy Place where the high priest could go once a year to make a sacrifice for the people.

Moses is told to put a veil as the divider between the Holy Place and the Most Holy Place. This veil, this barrier, separated the Levites from the presence of God. The Most Holy Place contained the Ark of the

Covenant which had the Ten Commandments, Aaron's rod, and a jar or manna. How cool is that?

These were reminders of God's provision and protection. On top of the Ark of the Covenant sat the cherubim (angels), who guarded the mercy seat (the middle) with their wings. Once a year, the high priest would sacrifice a bull first for himself and his family then sprinkle the blood over the mercy seat, which underscored that atonement was going to be God's way. Over and over, year after year, blood was spilt. It wasn't enough to cleanse the people. They keep sinning and continually need sacrifices and *atonement*, which is a fancy word for *reconciliation*.

But look at Ephesians 2 again (emphasis added)...
*"For He Himself is our peace, who has made us both one and has broken down **in His flesh** the dividing wall of hostility by abolishing the law of commandments expressed in ordinances, that he might create in himself one new man in place of the two, **so making peace,** and **might reconcile us** both to God in one body through the cross, **thereby killing the hostility."***

How did Jesus break down the wall?

It says *in His flesh* He broke down the wall of separation. Jesus made peace for us on the cross. He tore the curtain of the temple veil that kept the Levites from the presence of God.

The blue, purple, and scarlet thread of the temple veil are part of what makes this truth interesting. The Israelites learned how to make and sew this material while in captivity in Egypt! Skills they learned while in slavery would later be used to make the veil, their protection until the Prince of Peace came in the flesh.

Never discount your tough seasons! God doesn't waste anything. When things are hard, ask the Lord what He wants to show you. When you get to this new place, take the time to reflect on the ways God prepared you for His next step of obedience.

Spending regular time with Him, just like we need regular date nights with our husbands, helps us solidify and deepen the relationship. If we're not growing, we're dying. If we're not pressing in, we're pulling away. If we're not moving forward in a deepening affection for Him, we're letting our love grow cold.

Matthew 27:51 says,
"And behold, the curtain of the temple was torn in two, from top to bottom. And the earth shook, and the rocks were split."

The purpose of Jesus' coming in the flesh was so He could break down the dividing wall of hostility. The God of the universe made a way for us to be allowed in His presence!

GOD'S PRESENCE IS ACCESSIBLE TO YOU.

You don't need to be a high priest or wait for a special day to be in God's presence. You're not required to kill a bull before you can even walk into the room or wear special clothes to be with God. Because of Jesus, we have access to God's presence all the time.

It reminds me of the Ashley Craig pop song which says, *"Why don't you just meet me in the middle?"*[1] Isn't that the way we look at things with our human perspective? We think we need to clean up or make ourselves presentable before coming closer to God, believing we must meet Him in the middle. But God doesn't ask us to come halfway. *He comes all the way to us.* Jesus poured His own blood out for you on the mercy seat so you could have access to God. He did all the work.

GOD WANTS TO MEET WITH YOU, AND HE WANTS TO SPEAK TO YOU.

So what was the purpose of the Old Testament temple? What are we supposed to see in verse after verse of detailed building instructions?

In Exodus 25:22 God says,
"There I will meet with you and above the mercy seat I will speak with you."

Too often, more than I'd like to admit, I've thought of the Old Testament God as the one who's mean and mad – the bad cop who is out to deliver the Law. I thought of the New Testament God as the nice one who sent Jesus to pay our sin debt.

God is the same yesterday, today, and forever. His character or His heart toward us doesn't change between the Old and New Testaments. While we see the depth of our depravity more clearly and the harshness of the judgements we are due in the first half of the Bible – praise God – right here in Exodus, we see the simple truth that God desired to be with and speak with His people. Blows my mind every time. *"There I will meet with you and above the mercy seat I will speak with you."*

The name Prince of Peace in Isaiah and the principle that Jesus Himself is our peace in Ephesians, is something we can jump right over and miss. Tracing the "dividing wall" back to the Old Testament sends us on an adventure.

When it comes to your time in the Word, don't rush. Don't just check a box. You may experience days when it won't feel like you got anything and you may not get spiritual goosebumps. Keep pressing in. Go slow. Highlight the phrases that jump out at you and trace them throughout the rest of scripture. As He opens your eyes, let Him tell you where your feet should walk next. Make the commitment to spend time with God. He wants to be with you. He wants to speak to you.

10
FEET READY
WHAT WE BELIEVE IS IMPORTANT

To You, O God of my fathers, I give thanks and praise,
for You have given me wisdom and might, and have now made
known to me what we asked of You... – Daniel 2:23

IN THE WEEKS OF POSTPARTUM after my second child, I found myself shopping kid-free at H-E-B (Love them! It's a Texas thing!). With a list and pen in hand and the words "decaf coffee" next, I rounded the coffee aisle.

119

Inhale. *Ahhh.*

I skimmed the titles looking for H-E-B's Café Olé Texas Pecan. I heard such good things about this flavor. Instead of the regular San Antonio blend (also good, by the way) I grabbed a shiny black bag of Texas Pecan marked decaf and tossed it in the child's seat of the cart.

Fast forward a couple of days. I'm looking everywhere. I don't see the Texas Pecan. The bag is not in the coffee cupboard where I would have put it away. I look in the pantry. Nope. Calling out to Marcus, I asked him where in the world did he put my Texas Pecan when he was "helping" me unload the groceries. He says he doesn't remember seeing any coffee. I huff. I headed to the carport to inspect the back of the car. It must have been in a bag I left behind.

I hope there's nothing requiring refrigeration in the same bag.

I get to the car, pop the trunk. Nothing.

Darn it. The H-E-B cashier didn't give me all of my bags! What is this world coming to? How hard is it to make sure your customers have all of their groceries? Chase me down, give me my coffee. I'm slow enough in the parking lot; you could have caught up! Ughhh.

I grab my receipt, and I am about to call the phone number on the bottom to ask for a $7 refund for the coffee that did not make it home. Marcus heads outside to double-check the car for me.

Then all of a sudden, the pieces. The memories. They come flooding back. My cheeks turn bright red. I'm embarrassed.

So this is what it's like getting old.

Right on cue Marcus returns as I set the phone down.

"I put the coffee back," I say. Now, laughing at myself because of this situation, this case of "mom brain" is just too much to handle. How could I have forgotten my own choice?! *"I put the coffee back because I realized the decaf Texas Pecan was whole beans not ground, and I was too lazy to grind it at the store. I never bought the coffee."*

Now, I bet you've never *almost* called H-E-B to demand a refund. But I know I'm not the only one who has acted upon what I believed to be true. First, I believed Marcus had put the coffee away in the wrong spot. Then I believed he was irresponsible and had left a grocery bag in the car. Then I was convinced the store clerk was inept and had left a bag full and paid-for groceries in the spinning carousel to never make their way to my house. After all that, I was faced with the truth: I had put the wonderfully smelling Texas Pecan whole beans back on the shelf. I had not purchased any.

I didn't remember it. The memory loss was embarrassing, but it proves the point. **We will respond and act on what we believe to be true, which is why what we believe is so important.** I can't imagine the embarrassment that could have compounded if I'd continued to believe someone had taken my coffee then gotten a manager on the phone for a refund. The answer was right there in my hands. The receipt, though it had dozens of items listed, did not show a coffee purchase. There was no coffee in my cupboard because I did not purchase any.

What we believe to be true is important. We act on and respond to situations based on what we believe. We can be one-hundred percent wrong. We can forget the details and key pieces of information and still think we are right. We can blame our helpful husbands and the grocery store clerk and be completely off-base.

Our source for truth in life has to be ultimate. It can't be the opinions of people or on a human's fading memory. The basis for our decisions and our response to life need a foundation which lasts longer than these temporary sources. They can't bear the weight. The Bible is unlike any other book on the planet or in all of human history. It is without error. It is without contradiction. In the life of the believer, it has ultimate authority.

Yes, there have been people who have cherry-picked and chosen a verse out of context and tried to use it to bolster their own agendas. Like the sheep who know their Good Shepherd's voice and won't follow a stranger, we must be familiar with the *whole* Bible. It's not enough to check the pantry and find it empty to claim the bag is in the back of the car as true.

In today's "Google it" age, I fear for those who do not have familiarity with the entirety of God's Word and familiarity with the Spirit's voice. Hired hands who do not care for you when the wolves come in and start wreaking havoc on the Church live in our world. Their god is their belly and their glory is their shame. Their minds are set on earthly things (Philippians 3:19).

We can quickly ask the opinions of hundreds of our social media friends, but do we ever stop to ask the God who made us, consult the Bible, or trusted friends?

It's unpopular to say God is love, and He requires us to live holy (separate) lives. It's become counter to even the Christian subculture to say I can be kind and love *you* (someone in need of Jesus) without approving and condoning your unbiblical lifestyle.

It's not enough to believe the Bible and sit alone at home. All through scripture we see the value of friendships. Good, godly friendships with those who encourage us in our walk with the Lord and can challenge us to walk in obedience to the calling He has on our lives.

We need good friends who also seek to live in biblical truth who will pray and apply truth with us.

As we see with Daniel and his powerful prayer life, our relationship with God is about so much more than getting provision, protection, or relief. We need to have *both* a growing, healthy relationship with God and with a few, close friends who will pray with us. **God performs the truly miraculous and His name is glorified in this environment.**

In Daniel 2:17-30, God divinely answers the prayer of Daniel and his friends by revealing to Daniel the meaning of King Nebuchadnezzar's dream.

The king made a crazy decree that all of his wise men were to be put to death because no one could tell him *both* his dream and its interpretation. Daniel, in wisdom, hears this decree and asks if he can have an appointment with the king so he can give him an interpretation.

Take a moment to read this passage even if it's familiar to you.

"Then Daniel went to his house and made the matter known to Hananiah, Mishael, and Azariah, his companions, and told them to seek mercy from the God of heaven concerning this mystery, so that Daniel and his companions might not be destroyed with the rest of the wise men of Babylon. Then the mystery was revealed to Daniel in a vision of the night. Then Daniel blessed the God of heaven. Daniel answered and said:

'Blessed be the name of God forever and ever,
  to whom belong wisdom and might.
He changes times and seasons;
  he removes kings and sets up kings;
he gives wisdom to the wise
  and knowledge to those who have understanding;
he reveals deep and hidden things;
  he knows what is in the darkness,
  and the light dwells with him.
To you, O God of my fathers,
  I give thanks and praise,
for you have given me wisdom and might,
  and have now made known to me what we asked of you,
  for you have made known to us the king's matter.'"

Can you imagine Daniel coming home to his buddies that night? "Hey, guys. We need to pray for God to reveal the king's dream and it's meaning. If He doesn't, we're going to be put to death right alongside the rest of the Chaldeans and enchanters."

They pray together then **go to sleep!** They very well might be put to death tomorrow, and yet they have the peace of knowing they've asked the Lord. The future is in His hands. So they go to sleep. I can't imagine what the morning was like as they are all waking up, asking each other, "Did God reveal it to you?" "What about you?"

Then Daniel awakes and says, "God told me in a vision of the night!"

Daniel 2 continues:

"Therefore Daniel went into Arioch, whom the king had appointed to destroy the wise men of Babylon. He went and said thus to him: 'Do not

destroy the wise men of Babylon; bring me in before the king, and I will show the king the interpretation.'

Then Arioch brought in Daniel before the king in haste and said thus to him: 'I have found among the exiles from Judah a man who will make known to the king the interpretation.' The king declared to Daniel, whose name was Belteshazzar, 'Are you able to make known to me the dream that I have seen and its interpretation?' Daniel answered the king and said, 'No wise men, enchanters, magicians, or astrologers can show to the king the mystery that the king has asked, but there is a God in heaven who reveals mysteries, and he has made known to King Nebuchadnezzar what will be in the latter days. Your dream and the visions of your head as you lay in bed are these: To you, O king, as you lay in bed came thoughts of what would be after this, and he who reveals mysteries made known to you what is to be. But as for me, this mystery has been revealed to me, not because of any wisdom that I have more than all the living, but in order that the interpretation may be made known to the king, and that you may know the thoughts of your mind.'"

Daniel believed God would answer his prayer.
Daniel had a history of praying with his friends, even when it was against the rules. God had blessed them after their obedience to not defile themselves with the king's food and instead to eat vegetables and drink water. We see in Daniel 1:17,
"As for these youths, God gave them learning and skill in all literature and wisdom, and Daniel had understanding in all visions and dreams."

Daniel believed the credit belonged to God.
Only God knows what is coming next. Daniel knew it was not by his own wisdom that the mystery was made known. Daniel knew the revelation was God's doing. He honors God by telling the king, "It's not that I have more wisdom than all of the living, it's the God I

serve!" God used this moment to bring a pagan king to understand He alone is God. Later in verse 46, Nebuchadnezzar says,

"Truly, your God is God of gods and Lord of kings, and a revealer of mysteries, for you have been able to reveal this mystery."

He gives Daniel and his friends high honors, gifts, and positions in his government. If you're familiar with the book of Daniel, then you know one chapter later, Daniel's friends' faith is put to the test again in the fiery furnace. The faith of his friends was encouraged by this near-death experience when God miraculously came through for them through the obedience of Daniel.

Our God *is* the God of gods. There is no other way to Him. Not Buddhism, not Islam, not Mormonism, not Hindusim. Even King Nebuchadnezzar could not deny that Daniel's God, YHWH, the God of the Bible, is the God of gods.

"Truly, your God is God of gods and Lord of kings, and a revealer of mysteries, for you have been able to reveal this mystery."

ASKING IN FAITH

For me, one challenging aspect of prayer is the call to show sensitivity to God's overall purpose and plans. This isn't us trying to manipulate God. Praying God's will is our honest attempt to adjust our viewpoint to one sensitive to God's heart. It was not about Daniel saving his own skin. He prayed because he wanted to reveal the mystery to King Nebuchadnezzar. He saw God at work even in this pagan king's life and was ready and willing to be used by God to show Nebuchandnezzar the way to truth.

When we readjust to sync up with God's will as we pray, we are asking God to align our hearts with His purpose so we can truly ask for what He desires. So how else would God answer except to grant what we're asking? Daniel didn't say, "Save me and my friends from dying." I'm sure that was part of it, but he recognized God as the source of wisdom, might, knowledge, and understanding. He encouraged his friends to seek God in the midst of uncertainty. **We act in faith when we go to God first.** Faith pleases God (Hebrews 11:1).

LOOK UP

Let's stop looking horizontally (to our spouse, family, friends) for what can only come vertically (from God Himself). True, lasting relief and peace are not found in the words, "cancer free," "paid in full," or "you got the job." All of these things – health, material blessings, position – are temporary.

When I seek information, confirmation, or affirmation from mere earthly sources, I can expect mere earthly answers. It is not unlike King Nebuchadnezzar looking to the wise men of his day when he needed to consult the God of gods, the revealer of mysteries.

Often God uses moments of uncertainty and fear to draw us to Himself. God in His mercy had allowed the king to have a frightening dream he could not understand. God knew it would cause him to seek truth, and God also graciously provided Daniel to interpret the dream for him.

When my child has an unexplained rash, a sudden fever, can't sleep through the night, or won't potty train, who do I ask? First, I need to seek the wisdom of the Lord! He made my child. He knows the intricacies of every cell in their body, their fears, and their maturity level. He has the power to remove the fever, embolden the tentative, and give this mom some peace and love as I handle all the hurdles of parenting. Am I saying not to use modern medicine or conventional wisdom? No, but I am challenged to stay off Facebook (to horizontal sources) for potty training tips from my friends *before* I've spent time in prayer asking my God (vertical source) for wisdom on how to deal.

LOOK AROUND

Like Daniel, our true friends can play a role in helping us to seek the Lord first. What friends has He given you? Do you have people in your life who encourage your walk with the Lord? I think of Daniel as he came home after hearing the king's decree. He asked his three best friends and housemates to seek God's mercy on their behalf.

If you don't have someone in your life like that right now, what friendships can you pursue? Are you plugged-in at a Bible-believing church? Do they offer small groups or community groups where you can find friends?

When we moved from Houston to my hometown, it felt like starting over. My closest childhood friends had long since moved away. The nearest people around were ones who had babysat me as a child or wiped my bottom in the church nursery, so it was hard for them to see me as a grown-up with kids of my own. (Not even joking!) I missed the friends who'd known me as an adult, who I'd been growing with from a young newlywed of twenty-one, to the woman and mom I'd become.

God was so faithful to send me to First Baptist Church of San Antonio's MOPS group. These moms were my refuge. Our first year moving back was incredibly rough for me emotionally – handling a coilicy newborn, and not to mention our oldest broke his femur and was in a cast for several weeks. While in my season of blue, I read the book *Happiness is a Choice* by Frank Minirth and Paul Meier. In it, there was an assessment to score yourself by how much change had taken place in your life in the past year. I did the questionnaire and my score was off the charts. No wonder. It was hard right now because life *was* hard. It helped me give myself some grace. It gave me room to be vulnerable and be "normal" for feeling that way.

Through the course of our first year, I felt the tug to join the MOPS leadership team, which is where I began to deepen relationships, and my faith and personality were stretched. God had built my trust muscle personally as I sought new friendships, financially as my husband and I trusted Him to meet our needs as we started a business, and spiritually as I dug into the Word and served my fellow moms.

WORTH THE RISK

Trusting Him is worth the risk. It is worth the step of faith to say things out loud that might get you marked "religious" by some people. It's worth facing your fears to get to the end to say, "I did it. With God's help, I did it."

Riding a roller coaster is the way I described to a friend how it felt to go on stage at MOPS. I've shared a short devotional twice a month for two years to eighty moms, and I still feel the same way. Every. Single. Time.

A few minutes before I go up, I get a funny feeling deep in my stomach. The way you feel right before you're about to board a roller coaster. You've waited in line an hour for this, and you've seen the fifty-eight-second ride go by dozens of times. No one died. But you are still terrified.

Why did you sign up to do this?
You're not as prepared as you should be.
You really should let someone else do this.

The feeling of risk remains, so I continue to depend on God. I've learned to embrace it. Obedience is all about Him anyway. I am faithful to spend time with Him, seeking what He would have me say, and He is faithful to come through for me every time. Nervousness (and sometimes nausea!) is just part of the dance. I might fall. I might misspeak. I might get ahead of myself, talk way too fast and skip saying something I'd written down in my notes. But somehow, in the mess of it, He still figures out how to make it work.

Friends, that's because it was always Him doing the work. He invites us to join Him. He doesn't need us. He *wants* to partner with us. I don't understand it. But I don't question it anymore. Right beside me now I have the handwritten list of notes – statements I've had to say to myself through the course of writing this book, to remind myself of truth and to keep me writing in the midst of the doubts and fear that come when I leave this room and wonder why in the world I'm doing this.

God told me to do this.
God has given me things to say.
God has provided the tools and experience to move forward.
To stop would be to disobey.

I shared my list with Marcus, and he texted back something to add.

God wants to bless my obedience.

Cue the tears. What a beautiful picture of God's grace! He *wanted* to bless Daniel and his friends' obedience for avoiding the king's food. It made God's heart glad to show the king that Daniel was stronger than all the others on a diet of vegetables! He *wanted* to bless Daniel and his friends for seeking His face in the face of death for an interpretation to a dream they didn't even know. God used it all for His glory. That's how good He is.

Friends, when we put down our phones and allow God to open our eyes to the people and opportunities around us – amazing things can happen. When we face a problem by going to God first before asking for the counsel of the great and mighty Google search, we honor Him. When our feet are quick and ready to obey what He has asked us to do – what an opportunity it opens for Him to bless our obedience.

"He reveals deep and hidden things;
He knows what is in the darkness,
and the light dwells with Him."
Daniel 2:22

KENNAN BUCKNER

FEET READY

11

INFLUENCING IN THE NAME OF CHRIST

By this all people will know that you are My disciples,
if you have love for one another. – John 13:35

EARLY IN OUR MARRIAGE, I discovered Marcus is a "let it soak" kind of guy. Do you have one of those, too? It did not bother him a bit to take a tomato sauce covered pot, run some tap water over it with a splash of dish soap, and leave it in the sink overnight. I was surprised how moving in with just *one* person could make everything feel so messy!

I grew up with *shining* examples of structure and order. My Mom almost always cleared the kitchen before going to bed. It was a ritual. Every evening, my parents would finish whatever dishes were left, and then Dad would get tomorrow's coffee grounds and put them in the coffee pot before setting it for 5 a.m. Things were handled immediately.

Even my grandfather does this. The first thing after Sunday dinner, he, my grandmother, and my Aunt Denise go right to the kitchen and wash all the dishes. No one has ever heard of "letting it soak."

You see, Marcus and I have different ways of doing things. He had the idea that dishes were easier if they had time to soak. There was less scrubbing involved and less effort needed if he was patient to let Dawn do her job so he could do his later.

SEEING IT ON REPEAT

According to research, it takes about two months for a new habit to become automatic. When we do things a certain way over and over, the habit becomes ingrained in us, which is how our phone habits formed. According to the *New York Post*, "Americans check their phone on average once every 12 minutes – burying their heads in their phones 80 times a day, according to new research. A study by global tech protection and support company Asurion found that the average person struggles to go little more than 10 minutes without checking their phone."[1]

This habitual need to check what is happening online means we are not as available to those who are physically around us as we should be. In the Gospel of John, we get a peek into the life of the disciples when Jesus tells them He wants them to be known by one identifier: love.

In thinking about the idea of what makes Christians different, I keep running into John 13:12-35 when Jesus washes His disciples-feet during what we call the Last Supper. He warns them a betrayer lives among them, and then He gives out what He calls a "new" commandment. His commandment: love one another. This wasn't really new. The disciples had been taught to love God and others since they were little. So why was Jesus calling this a *new* command?

John Piper points out earlier in chapter 13, John says Jesus "loved them to the end" or to the uttermost.[3] Jesus loves them to the full. Then He shows or demonstrates this ultimate love by laying aside his status and privileges and washing their feet. This was something a servant should have done before they started dinner. Instead of calling out the host, or pointing at one of the disciples and giving them the task of scrubbing no-doubt sandy, dirty feet, He did it. This new level of servanthood was going to become a tangible reminder for them of what God's love looks like.

As moms, we get this opportunity to lay aside our plans and privileges – to serve and love to the uttermost almost every day, don't we? When relationships don't feel 50/50 or when it's not "my" turn to do such and such, I can choose to take the form of a servant. Like my Jesus, I can love just like this new command from my Savior.

Jesus says, *"This is how people will know you are mine: by the way you love."* (John 13:35)

Love is what makes Christianity different! Christianity is a relationship. It's not only morality. Our access to God is not based on rituals or our achievements, self-denial, or spiritual knowledge. The basis of the relationship is love. Put more accurately: *His love for us.* We love Him because He first loved us (1 John 4). Jesus tells His disciples this love He has for them is the love they can have for others.

THE POWER OF LOVING OTHERS

1. You are an influencer.
You may not have thousands of followers on your social media accounts, but you are an influencer because of love.

In 2 Timothy 1:5, Paul reminds Timothy of the influence his grandmother and mother had on his faith and his walk. These words are a reminder to us of the power of influence we've been given.

"I am reminded of your sincere faith, a faith that dwelt first in your grandmother Lois and your mother Eunice and now, I am sure, dwells in you as well."

Generational impact is at stake here. Have you thought about your kids' kids? I don't know about you, but I can't think past elementary school! I can't picture my kids driving, having jobs, let alone getting married and having children of their own. But here it is right there in the Bible: through the power of love, we can pass down our faith.

Early childhood development experts from First Things First say newborn brains grow at a rate of one percent a day and by age five, ninety percent of a child's brain development has occurred.[2] That is amazing! It puts into perspective how precious our time with our kids is.

I was reading more about this and came across an article in the *Washington News*. It turned into one of those "Don't ask me why I'm crying" moments because God used it to speak to me. I had a good private cry right there with my laptop in my room post bedtime.

Here's what it said, "If we're all going to live as long as they say we're going to live, then you have many, many years to be high-achieving in your profession – to make lots of money, to have great material success – but you really have a very short time to have this critical influence on your children's emotional well-being."[3]

Your presence matters! Your time is short! Whether you work full-time or part-time, or stay at home, we know our phones can steal us from embracing the present. We mindlessly scroll. We can't stop checking notifications every few minutes. We have got to put down our phones, forget the likes and shares, turn off the television, and be there with our kids! Get on the floor, snuggle with them, read to them, play games with them, enjoy them.

High-achieving moms, we struggle with this! I know when one of my three goes down for a nap, I say, "Time to boost our productivity!" and I'm off to accomplish a list of house chores in a frenzied don't-get-in-my-way attitude. Instead, I need to relax. Take a deep breath. Leave the Notes app with its lists. And realize the opportunity I have been given to make an impact that will last generations.

These little people are *people*. They have eternal souls. They have unique perspectives. They are taking everything in and absorbing it! They need to know they are loved by us and by God. **They need to be able to come to their parents without having to compete with our phones for our attention.** They need to know what's most important to us is our relationship with God and with them.

Let's be moms whose kids know they are more precious to us than answering a text, scrolling Facebook, or posting smiling photos of them for friends to see. Let's be moms who care more about our people than a crumb-free kitchen floor, emptied dishwasher, or folded laundry.

What I want them to remember is what a joy I thought they were. What a treasure it was to get to spend time with them. What fun I had being with them today.

I want the sincere faith Paul talked about to be evident in my life, so my kids can mirror it in theirs. I cannot wait to see what God does in their lives, to become a grandma, and to have my grandkids over. Influencing others through the love of Jesus is an opportunity with generational potential.

Practically speaking, because our three kids are still so young, most of the house upkeep is still done by us, although I am plotting when a chore chart will be part of life! I have learned to accept that the dishwasher loading and unloading is now a daily task as a family of five, which was a hard one for me! I have also decided to leave the living room a wreck during the day. I am tempted to put away the one basket of toys that keeps getting dumped and spread around, but friend, the basket will be re-dumped and re-spread in a matter of minutes. So I wait until my husband starts the bedtime routine to scoop up the toys from the floors and load the dishwasher from the day of eating and drinking. I celebrate my hitting the "Clean" button on my vacuuming robot before heading off to bed. I'm spoiled. I know.

Want another Buckner lifehack? We dress our kids for church on Saturday night after bathtime. Yep. They sleep in their church clothes. Have you ever tried to wrangle three youngsters who somehow know it's the one day you all need to be somewhere at a certain time? I feel like Macus and I are chasing cats to wrestle their clothes on. Our kids are not immune to whining, fussing, and slower-than-a-sloth movement. So, we decided to skip the whole pajama thing. We dress them the night before when they're more compliant. It builds anticipation for what's coming the next day, and it gets their minds prepared for attending church. Our oldest loves calling his collared shirts his "church shirts," and it's so cute to hear him say it. So there's that.

2. You will be known by a lot of things.

The truth is we Christians are known for a lot of things. Sometimes we are known more for what we are *against* than what we are *for*. I can't tell you how many political or religious arguments I have seen take place on social media or via email forwards. I wonder sometimes if important issues are ever resolved through online arguments.

What *should* we be known for?

Here are a few things:

Ephesians 4:32 *"Be kind to one another, tenderhearted, forgiving one another, as God in Christ forgave you."*

Philippians 2:4 *"Have the mind in you that is humble and counts others more significant than yourselves and looks not only to your own interests but also to the interests of others."*

Titus 2:3-5 *"Older women likewise are to be reverent in behavior, not slanderers or slaves to much wine. They are to teach what is good, and so train the young women to love their husbands and children, to be self-*

controlled, pure, working at home, kind, and submissive to their own husbands, that the word of God may not be reviled."

1 Peter 3:3-4 *"Do not let your adorning be external – the braiding of hair and the putting on of gold jewelry, or the clothing you wear – but let your adorning be the hidden person of the heart with the imperishable beauty of a gentle and quiet spirit, which in God's sight is very precious."*

As we stop to consider not only our interests, but also the interests of our two-year-olds, we love our husbands and children well and Christ is honored.

FOCUS ON THE FIRSTS

One way to be known by the way we love is to think of your family's firsts and to make focused attention a priority during those key moments. The first time you see each family member after you wake up, the first time you see each other after being apart – like when someone comes home from work or school – and when you put your kids down for bed.

Because we are self-employed and I have been a stay-at-home/work-mostly-from-home mom the past five years, I sleep in until 7 a.m. I know it's a luxury because in my mid-20s I was leaving the house in business casual at 7 a.m. for a 50-minute commute.

Sometimes, my boys get up before me. When they do, they climb in bed with me for conversation and attention. My oldest loves telling me what he dreamed about the night before. While I try to start my day with my YouVersion Bible app before moving to other notifications, emails, etc. I know to them – mommy looking at her phone is mommy looking at her phone.

Sometimes I'll tell them what Bible verse I am reading, or what truth I am learning. Other times, as soon as I see them peering in the door, I'll tuck the phone under the covers and be ready for lots of eye contact and snuggles. The point is, I focus on those first encounters. I want my body language and the tone of my voice to communicate love. If the first thing I do when I see them in the morning is "Shhhh," order them out of the room, or ignore their stories by not looking at them with my eyes, I am communicating instead *You are an interruption. You are not important to me. You are not wanted here.* None of us would ever want our little people to feel that way. We know the weight of greetings and the way they can make us feel included, wanted, and special. Let's be moms who greet our people with love. Even if you are not a "morning person," you can still be kind. The firsts matter.

3. You can only love as well as you know you are loved.

I used to hear the list of the fruits of the Spirit in Galatians 5 and think of it as a list of admirable traits to aspire to, but I missed the entire point. We can't have love, joy, peace, patience, kindness, goodness, faithfulness, gentleness, and self-control apart from the Spirit.

When I'm struggling to be patient I don't need to try harder to be patient, I need to be with Jesus! John Piper says in the passage in John where Jesus washes his disciples' feet "draws attention not only to the *pattern* of love we follow, but the *power* to love that we need."[4]

He is our source. The more we are bathed in His love, the greater capacity we have to love others. Our relationship is not based on rule-keeping love – an outside force trying to control the inside – but transformed from the inside out kind of love. That's what is new.

One fun thing to do is to put your name in scripture. John 15:9-10 says, *"As the Father has loved me, so have I loved you, _____. Abide in my love. If you, _____ , keep my commandments, you will abide in my love, just as I have kept my Father's commandments and abide in his love."*

Like my husband's dishes need to soak to get off the grime, I need to soak in the love of Jesus if I am ever going to love my people like He wants me to. It won't come by trying harder.

FINDING A PLACE TO SOAK

You can weave tactical practices into normal life to allow you these soaking moments. Tish Harrison Warren says in *Liturgy of the Ordinary: Sacred Practices in Everyday Life,* "The kind of spiritual life and disciplines needed to sustain the Christian life are quiet, repetitive, and ordinary. I often want to skip the boring, monotonous stuff to get to the thrill of an edgy faith. But it's in the dailiness of the Christian faith – the making the bed, the doing the dishes, the praying for our enemies, the reading the Bible, the quiet, the small – that God's transformation takes root and grows."[5]

Write scripture verses on notecards and place them around your home where you will see them – on the bathroom mirror, by the diaper changing table, inside the pantry door. When you're washing the dishes and they are yucky and stinky and you don't know why it's "your turn" again, remember He said whatever we do for the least, we do for Him. We can wash dishes with cheerfulness... for Him.

Make one day a week a screen-free day. Go somewhere (run an errand, go for a walk, visit a friend) without taking your phone. When you find yourself looking horizontally for the vertical kind of love and approval you need, tell Him. Take time to read a book of the Bible repetitively. Maybe try a translation you've never read before. Listen to encouraging music or scripture-focused podcasts. Tend to your soul before turning to screens.

Remember God is with you. Three kids ages five and under is no joke. Before you put me on some sort of spiritual pedestal, let me tell you: I still lose it. I don't always exercise the fruit of self-control from the Holy Spirit. When my boys are fighting with each other (with boys it somehow always turns physical!) I pray out loud as I separate them. *Lord, help us to use our hands for good. God, help us to have self-control.* Inviting Jesus into my parenting, audibly, in front of the ones I am seeking to parent counts as the two or more who are gathered (Matthew 18:20).

Remember what Piper said, Jesus is the *pattern* of love to follow and the *power* to love? Self-dependence will end in failure. Human strength will run out. Even you will get tired and weary (Isaiah 40:30-31). But He will not fail you. His redemptive power is so great that when you do fail, He can still turn it into something good. What God invites you to is a *daily* walk, with *daily* bread.

> Looking for a podcast? My editor Jill E. McCormick hosts **Grace In Real Life** where you will find grace-filled reminders of God's love. Find it on iTunes or Spotify.

As an introvert whose motherly duties mean I rarely get to be alone, I love long car rides because I have time to think and process. I often tune in to podcasts while I drive. I soak in the love of God during my quiet drives alone. I have podcast subscriptions to several sermon series, talented speakers, and authors on my phone right now.

Phones are not bad. They are tools. So many apps keep the Word at the forefront of our minds. There's the *First 5* app with free daily devotionals, the *YouVersion* app with Bible reading plans and devotionals, and the list goes on. Our devices don't have to distract us from what is ultimate; they are tools we can use to draw near to God.

In our MOPS group, someone once brought scripture verses printed in stylish typography for us to have. These notecard-sized scriptures are taped throughout my house. I've got one on the refrigerator, one inside the pantry door, one by the thermostat, one by the diaper changing table, another on my bathroom mirror. Wherever I look throughout my day, I have the heavenly reminders of truth.

FOLLOWING HIS LEAD

We can only pass on the love we experience ourselves. It's funny how God uses the lessons we want to teach our children to teach us! My husband puts our boys to bed. They share a bedroom now, and Marcus lies with them for a few minutes, reads a story, then they sing and pray.

Our oldest son, Jaxson, is learning about prayer from those experiences, and sometimes he wants to pray aloud, too. One evening, he decided he wanted to pray for a marble run set. You see, earlier in the day, Marcus showed him YouTube videos of one because he had played with a marble run set as a kid.

If you have ever been around a kid like ours, you know they can sometimes fixate on certain things. Well, a marble run set was his new fixation. He began to pray for one every night. He asked and begged for us to buy him one, but with a quick search on Amazon it was clear, it was not in our budget right now.

Jaxson was convinced they needed to go to our thrift store, because they would find a marble run set there. He had prayed. So it was going to happen.

We tried to preemptively soften the blow. You know. Lower his expectations. (Real good Christian parenting, right?) We said, "You know, sometimes when we pray for things God says no, or He says wait. It doesn't always work out the way we ask."

The next day, the boys load up to go to the thrift store. They'd been gone for a while, and Marcus texts me while they're there. He sends me a picture with no words. All I could say back was, "What is that?" Tears rush down my face. The photo was a picture of a marble run set in a giant plastic bag. The boys had already searched the whole thrift store, found nothing they wanted, and were about to leave. Marcus said that by the front door was this bag. And in it? Y'all, I am crying as I type this. It was a marble run set. For $3. At our local thrift store. In a town of 4,000 people.

There. Is. No. Way. There is no other explanation than God put it there because a little boy prayed in faith. It was God's great and precious and good pleasure to give Jaxson what he had asked for. Marcus was overcome standing there in the thrift store. He started to cry, too, and told Jaxson, "See how much God loves you!"

Friends, I have a picture of Jaxson playing with the marble run set when they got it home. I posted it on our kitchen memo board. It serves to remind me. See how much He cares!

What God wanted to say to me was:
ASK ME.
BELIEVE ME.
LOOK FOR ME.

My sweet Jaxson will have a personal story of God's faithfulness to carry with him his whole life. And I will have a story to carry with me throughout mine.

Every day is not a blog entry. Today is Monday, and I cannot find an Instagram-worthy photo to share on my camera roll. Sometimes our influence and the "new" command of loving others can feel like a long and unrewarding grind, but praise God for those bright glimpses that remind us He is working! His way of parenting and living and loving is what is best for us, our families, our communities, and our world.

Keep your chin up. Put your phone down. Open your eyes. Ready your feet for the path He has for you. There is no other better adventure.

SMALL GROUP DISCUSSION GUIDE

PHONE DOWN
Chapter 1: No More Fear of Missing Out
- Pick one or two of the decision statements from the chapter that stand out to you, adopt them, and share yours with the group.
- What FOMO have you experienced recently? What is the truth?

Chapter 2: Anticipate the Blessing
- Desperation can reveal who/what you really count on. What have you been desperate for lately?
- Where did you turn in your most recent crisis? (Inward, outward, or upward?)
- Where do you anticipate God working? How are you preparing for His blessing?

Chapter 3: What We Need to Remember
- What was one of your earliest memories with your spouse?
- What are some methods you use to remember things? (Calendar on your phone, sticky notes, scrapbooks?)
- Share something God has done in your life you want to remember.

Chapter 4: We are His Workmanship
- What gifts and abilities has God given you? What do people tell you you're good at?
- What talents do you need to press into, learn more about, and how could you use them for God's Kingdom?
- Where do you see God at work, and how can you join in?

EYES OPEN
Chapter 5: Building Your God-Confidence
- Just as God revealed Himself as "The Lord is Peace" to Gideon

before the battle, when has the Lord given you exactly what you needed?

- What can you say to encourage the Gideons in your world to affirm the gifts and calling God has on their lives?
- Gideon was told to destroy the family altars for the false god Baal. Are there stands you need to take in your family and community? Gideon earned a nickname because of his stand. Have you already earned some nicknames?

Chapter 6: Do Not Harden Your Heart
- Are you allowing things to harden you or refine you? What shapes your perspective?
- What hard, tough, or annoying things in your life right now could be used by God to soften you?
- If the current you (attitudes, actions, and reactions) were turned into the 100-year-old you, who would you be?

Chapter 7: Remembering Whose We Are
- Who do you listen to? Who or what are your trusted sources for truth?
- In what areas have you left the Good Shepherd's protection and put yourself under a hired hand?
- Read John 10:9-16. Have you walked through the door? If so, you'll know because the Good Shepherd is leading you in and out to find good pasture.

Chapter 8: This is the Day the Lord Has Made
- As you think of Psalm 118:24, how does context change your perspective on *why* we rejoice?
- Let's rejoice together. Share about a joyful time in your life.
- As you trace the way you came to faith (the person who told the

person who told you) how does knowing it was always God's plan to rescue you "marvelous" in your eyes?

Pray: *What have I built upon besides You? Some days are not happy and life is hard. Let it be marvelous in my eyes knowing it was Your plan, purpose, and idea all along to rescue me. You are the cornerstone. You determine the position of my entire life. I fix my eyes on You, and that is what allows me to rejoice and be glad in this day You have made.*

FEET READY

Chapter 9: Our Prince of Peace

- Do you have "instant replay" moments when you fail?
- How has your view of God changed since you were a new Christian? How has it changed since you were in middle school? How did you view Him in your early 20s?
- Read Exodus 25:22 again. What do you think about the fact that God wants to meet with you and to speak to you?
- If you are comfortable, share personal prayer requests with your group.

Chapter 10: What We Believe is Important

- Share about a time in your life when God answered a prayer request. Be bold and specific.
- Share about a time when you believed something that wasn't true, but you acted on it. (Maybe you had your own coffee-you-didn't-actually-buy moment!)
- Do you have any friends like Daniel? Share how you plan to connect with them soon.

Chapter 11: Influencing in the Name of Christ

- Who is someone who influenced you as a child and how?
- What is one way you want to be known by love this week?

- Share a time when you really soaked in God's love. How can you implement soaking into your normal routine?

Pray: *Thank You for Your compassion. You chose to eat with sinners, and You made religious people mad. You commanded the disciples to do as You had done. You're not asking us to do anything You haven't done Yourself. Impress on us with Your Holy Spirit when we are not doing the right thing, or when we are doing what is right, but we are not doing it in love. Remind us how much You love us. Amen.*

HOW TO BECOME A CHRISTIAN

From sbc.net/knowjesus/theplan.asp

You're not here by accident. God loves you. He wants you to have a personal relationship with Him through Jesus, His Son. There is just one thing that separates you from God. That one thing is sin.

The Bible describes sin in many ways. Most simply, sin is our failure to measure up to God's holiness and His righteous standards. We sin by things we do, choices we make, attitudes we show, and thoughts we entertain. We also sin when we fail to do right things. The Bible affirms our own experience – "there is none righteous, not even one." No matter how good we try to be, none of us does right things all the time.

People tend to divide themselves into groups – good people and bad people. But God says that every person who has ever lived is a sinner, and that any sin separates us from God. No matter how we might classify ourselves, this includes you and me. We are all sinners.

"For all have sinned and come short of the glory of God." Romans 3:23
Many people are confused about the way to God. Some think they will be punished or rewarded according to how good they are. Some think they should make things right in their lives before they try to come to God. Others find it hard to understand how Jesus could love them when other people don't seem to. But I have great news for you! God DOES love you! More than you can ever imagine! And there's nothing you can do to make Him stop! Yes, our sins demand punishment – the punishment of death and separation from God. But, because of His great love, God sent His only Son Jesus to die for our sins.

"God demonstrates His own love for us in this: While we were still sinners, Christ died for us." Romans 5:8

For you to come to God you have to get rid of your sin problem. But, in our own strength, not one of us can do this! You can't make yourself right with God by being a better person. Only God can rescue us from our sins. He is willing to do this not because of anything you can offer Him, but JUST BECAUSE HE LOVES YOU!

"He saved us, not because of righteous things we had done, but because of His mercy." Titus 3:5

It's God's grace that allows you to come to Him – not your efforts to "clean up your life" or work your way to Heaven. You can't earn it. It's a free gift.

"For it is by grace you have been saved, through faith – and this not from yourselves, it is the gift of God – not by works, so that no one can boast." Ephesians 2:8-9

For you to come to God, the penalty for your sin must be paid. God's gift to you is His son, Jesus, who paid the debt for you when He died on the Cross.

"For the wages of sin is death, but the gift of God is eternal life in Jesus Christ our Lord." Romans 6:23

Jesus paid the price for your sin and mine by giving His life on a cross at a place called Calvary, just outside of the city walls of Jerusalem in ancient Israel. God brought Jesus back from the dead. He provided the way for you to have a personal relationship with Him through Jesus. When we realize how deeply our sin grieves the heart of God and how desperately we need a Savior, we are ready to receive God's offer of salvation. To admit we are sinners means turning away from our sin and selfishness and turning to follow Jesus. The Bible word for this is "repentance" – to change our thinking about how grievous sin is, so our thinking is in line with God's.

All that's left for you to do is to accept the gift that Jesus is holding out for you right now.

"If you confess with your mouth, "Jesus is Lord," and believe in your heart that God raised him from the dead, you will be saved. For it is with your heart that you believe and are justified, and it is with your mouth that you confess and are saved." Romans 10:9-10

God says that if you believe in His son, Jesus, you can live forever with Him in glory.

"For God so loved the world that He gave his one and only Son, that whoever believes in him shall not perish, but have eternal life." John 3:16

Are you ready to accept the gift of eternal life that Jesus is offering you right now? Let's review what this commitment involves:

- I acknowledge I am a sinner in need of a Savior – this is to repent or turn away from sin

- I believe in my heart that God raised Jesus from the dead – this is to trust that Jesus paid the full penalty for my sins

- I confess Jesus as my Lord and my God – this is to surrender control of my life to Jesus

- I receive Jesus as my Savior forever – this is to accept that God has done for me and in me what He promised

If it is your sincere desire to receive Jesus into your heart as your personal Lord and Savior, then talk to God from your heart:

Here's a Suggested Prayer:
"Lord Jesus, I know that I am a sinner and I do not deserve eternal life. But, I believe You died and rose from the grave to make me a new creation and to prepare me to dwell in your presence forever. Jesus, come into my life, take control of my life, forgive my sins and save me. I am now placing my trust in You alone for my salvation and I accept your free gift of eternal life."

If you have trusted Jesus as your Lord and Savior, please let me know. I want to rejoice in what God has done in your life and help you to grow spiritually by connecting with a local church.

If you have questions or concerns you would like help with (if I don't know we can reach out to trusted pastors and Christian leadership to find out together), please contact me and let me know. Email me at kennan.buckner@gmail.com or find a community of friends on Facebook in the group "Chin Up the Book."

NOTES
Chapter 2
[1]Spurgeon, Charles. The Complete Works of C. H. Spurgeon, Volume 13: Sermons 728 to 787, Fort Collins, Colorado, Delmarva Publications, Inc., 2015

Chapter 4
[1]Jensen, C. James. 7 KEYS To Unlock Your Full Potential, Cardiff-by-the-Sea, California, Waterside Publications, 2015

[2]Blackaby Henry, Claude V. King, and Richard Blackaby Experiencing God: Knowing and Doing the Will of God, Nashville, Tennessee, B&H Publishing Group, 2008

[3]Singleton, Laura. Grace: Hammock or Slingshot blog, 2012. https://blogs.bible.org/grace-hammock-or-slingshot/

[4]Wright, Christy. There's Room for You Too blog, 2014 https://www.christywright.com/articles/theres-room-for-you-too

Chapter 5
[1]King, Ross. "Clear the Stage," Ross King Music, 2002

Chapter 6
[1]Mckelvey, Doug / Gray, Jason / Ingram, Jason. "Nothing Is Wasted" Spirit Music Group, Essential Music Publishing, Capitol Christian Music Group, Music Services, Inc.

Chapter 7
[1]Tozer, A.W. The Knowledge of the Holy Fig, 1968

Chapter 9
[1]Jordan Johnson / Anton Zaslavski / Stefan Adam Johnson / Michael G. Trewartha / Kyle Mark Trewartha / Sarah Paige Aarons / Marcus Lamax "The Middle" lyrics © Universal Music Corp., Sony/atv Songs Llc, Zedd Music Empire, Songs Of Universal Inc., Aggressively Average Songs

Chapter 11
[1]New York Post https://nypost.com/2017/11/08/americans-check-their-phones-80-times-a-day-study/

[2]First Things First https://www.firstthingsfirst.org/early-childhood-matters/brain-development/

[3]Nania, Rachel. Washington News https://wtop.com/parenting/2017/05/why-prioritizing-motherhood-in-the-first-three-years-is-critical/

[4]Piper, John https://www.desiringgod.org/messages/the-new-commandment-of-christ-love-one-another-as-i-have-loved-you

[5]Warren, Tish Harrison. Liturgy of the Ordinary: Sacred Practices in Everyday Life InterVarsity Press 2016

Made in the USA
Monee, IL
28 September 2020